AGAINST ALL ODDS

*"Lord, I've ruined my life.
I'm Yours, if You still want me."*

JIM STIER

P.O. BOX 55787   SEATTLE, WA 98155

YWAM Publishing is the publishing ministry of Youth With A Mission. Youth With A Mission (YWAM) is an international missionary organization of Christians from many denominations dedicated to presenting Jesus Christ to this generation. To this end, YWAM has focused its efforts in three main areas: 1) Training and equipping believers for their part in fulfilling the Great Commission (Matthew 28:19). 2) Personal evangelism. 3) Mercy ministry (medical and relief work).

For a free catalog of books and materials write or call:

YWAM Publishing
P.O. Box 55787, Seattle, WA 98155
(425) 771-1153 or (800) 922-2143
www.ywampublishing.com

Publisher's Cataloging-in-Publication
(Provided by Quality Books, Inc.)

Stier, Jim.
    Against all odds / Jim Stier. -- 2nd ed.
    p. cm. -- (International adventures)
    ISBN: 0-927545-44-6

    1. Missions--Brazil. 2. Missionaries--Brazil.
I. Title.

BV2853.B6S75 2000   266.02373081
                 QBI00-500149

Against All Odds

Published by YWAM Publishing
P.O. Box 55787, Seattle, WA 98155

ISBN 0-927545-44-6

Printed in the United States of America.

Other International Adventures

Acknowledgments

W R I T I N G a book is definitely a team effort, and I would like to acknowledge the members of that team.

A special and overwhelming thanks goes to Janice Rogers, my editor. I knew nothing about writing a book, and she painstakingly led me through a basic course of instruction in the midst of the project. When instruction wasn't enough, she spent long days of work fixing the manuscript. This never could have happened without her.

A special thanks is also due to Jim Rogers, Janice's husband and also a member of the editing team. He kept us at work and made many invaluable suggestions.

There were also many others who read, edited, suggested changes, and contributed in many ways to this project: Lucy Allen, Nancy Boerman, Sharon Brookshire, Phyllis Griswold, Jim Shaw, and Pam Warren. A special thanks to Jimi Miller for the use of her home during the editorial process. Thank you all.

Also there were those who lived through many of the events included in this book, and who read through the manuscript to help us make sure our facts were right. Gerson and Elisa Ribeiro, Jaime and Maristela Araújo, Pam Stier, Marcelo and Rosane Machado, and George and Dolly Foster all helped out on this, and we thank them.

I dedicate this book to Pam, my wife. If there is a hero in this book, it is Pam. The victories wouldn't have been possible without her dedication, faith, and courage.

Contents

Preface

L I F E with Jesus is difficult, interesting, and wonderful. It
is an error to think that difficulties are always bad, or that prosperous,
abundant ease is always good. Jesus said that whoever loves his life in
this world will lose it, and whoever loses his life for His sake and for
the sake of the gospel will find it.

In these pages you will find a story of great difficulties and of wonderful victories. The people involved often failed, but by God's grace
they managed to keep to the right course. Jesus' words came true.

My prayer for you is that you might find your life, and that this
book might be of some help to you in that quest.

Introduction

THIS was no sophisticated, well-prepped missionary team. At best, it was a ragtag group of seventeen young people bound for Africa to save souls.

Even the routine sights at Rio's international airport thrilled them. Every experience was new, and they greeted each as a once-in-a-lifetime adventure. One girl pushed her luggage cart, piled high with baggage, onto the down escalator. The nose of the cart began to tip, and someone below shouted a warning. People jumped off in every direction as the load submitted to gravity and gathered momentum. An avalanche of totes, duffels, and bedrolls tumbled down the moving staircase.

Another young couple noticed a sign with large letters: "Concourse C." They didn't read the small print but jumped over a low platform and wandered through a labyrinth of hallways, emerging at Concourse C. They had climbed over the scale for oversized luggage and gone through a restricted area, arriving in the international lounge without submitting to passport control! This escapade practically touched off an international incident among the security staff and federal police who, after an animated lecture, finally forgave them and stamped their passports.

A team member with an overload of baggage attempted to squeeze through a security gate with all his gear. The guards yelled, "Stop! Stop! The conveyor belt!" The young man misunderstood, jumped on the conveyor belt, and proceeded through the X-ray machine.

It was like *The Marx Brothers Go to Africa,* and my friends were the zany cast. I smiled. They weren't the most serene missionaries ever commissioned for a tough field assignment, but they were among the most courageous.

I worried about them. They had raised as much support as possible from the Brazilian church, but the amount wouldn't meet their most basic needs. They would have to live at a bare survival level in Africa. We had already been warned that diseases ran rampant where they were headed, and we knew that virtually no medical facilities or doctors would be on hand to help.

I feared for my young friends. I prayed for them. And, oddly enough, I envied them. How well I remembered when Pam and I were their age, about to embark on the most wonderful, frightening, dangerous adventure of our lives.

Our experience, like theirs, had begun in this same airport. We, too, had been young, inexperienced, and without adequate monthly support. We had known no Portuguese, our one-way tickets hadn't included visas, and our pocket money had amounted to $3 in cash and a $60 check. One major difference separated our situation from theirs. Instead of exuding this group's blind faith, I had been plagued by insecurity and questions. I never doubted God, but I often doubted myself. I remember depending on Pam, my bride of eleven months, for assurance.

"Are you okay?" she had asked me when we arrived here so many years ago. I had replied with a litany of potential problems, most of them beginning with the words "What if...?" She answered my questions with two of her own.

"Don't you believe God told us to come?"

I nodded, remembering all that God had done to bring us to that point.

"So, why are you worried?"

She would repeat her questions often during our early years as missionaries. *Don't you believe God told us to come? So, why are you worried?* However, my insecurities were deeply rooted in a difficult and lonely childhood, and it would take years for me to acquire the confidence that came so easily to my wife and to this merry band of believers headed for Africa.

But it would happen—it *did* happen—because it was all part of God's plan...and my story.

Abandoned!

D A R K N E S S was settling in by the time our school bus wound its way through the desert toward our trailer park. The school was ninety minutes away, and I was tired and grumpy. Why had we moved to Utah? I missed California so much. I shut my eyes and envisioned my friends, the trout streams, and our two-story house in the middle of the grove of big pine trees.

I even had my own money back in Burney. I had worked cleaning the local movie theaters—the indoor theater in the winter and the drive-in theater in the summer. Each day after I finished, I was rewarded with a root-beer float, Beeman's gum, and a quarter.

My dad had owned the local Shell gas station. On weekends I went with him in the frosty mornings to open up. Usually we were the first ones on Main Street. I loved having Dad all to myself as we sat inside the warm service station waiting for the first customers. Everyone liked Dad. He was handsome and had an easy smile, and his prematurely gray hair swept back from a widow's peak. People trusted him. I wished he had never sold the station; I wished we'd never left Burney.

But we had, and several families made the move with us. None of them had any kids my age, except for our friends, Jack and Lucille, and they just had girls. Sometimes I'd go over there to play. I was always careful to behave myself. Lucille was a big, strong woman with an Oklahoma accent and a direct manner. I didn't want to upset her.

The bus slowed down as we neared the trailer park. I got out and trudged toward our mobile home, wishing one more time that it were our big house in Burney. My sisters were at the playground, taking advantage of the last bit of fading light. Did they hate it here as much as I did? I went inside, not realizing that the next few minutes would signal a change that would affect the rest of our lives.

It was gloomy as I walked into the tiny living room. Mom sat alone in the shadows. "What's going on, Mom?" I asked. "Something wrong?" I flipped on the light switch. Her brownish-blond hair hung over her eyes, and as she brushed it away, I saw the tears.

"Go to the store and get some boxes, Jim."

"Why? How come you're crying?"

"We're going back to California. We have to pack our things."

I paused in surprise, partly at the news and partly at her reaction to it. "But that's great! Why are you crying?"

"Because your dad isn't going with us. He doesn't want us anymore."

For a moment I stood motionless. How could this be? My parents never argued. In Burney I had known only one girl whose folks were divorced, and she seemed like some kind of oddity. Could this be happening? No, I wouldn't let it! I screamed and stomped around the trailer, blinded by tears. "No! No! No!"

Mom jumped up from the couch and ran to hold me. "Jim, be quiet. Everyone will hear you." She brushed the tears from my cheeks. I stopped crying and pushed her away. I dashed outside into the darkened desert. I needed to be alone and think through my mother's awful announcement.

After a few minutes I was shivering with emotion and the cold. I blinked away tears and looked back toward the lights of our trailer house. Of course, it wasn't true. We were a family. I clenched my jaw and fists as I headed back. I told myself it would all work out.

Nothing more was said, but during the next few days, I began to notice small clues that I had missed before. Dad was spending more and more time at Lucille's house. And when he was home, he and Mom hardly spoke to each other. I could feel the tension. Then one day a little hope came into my heart. My parents called my two sisters and me into the living room for a family conference.

"Some people still owe us money for our house and service station in Burney," Dad explained. "You kids are going back with Mom and take care of wrapping up the business. I'll come and pick you up later when it's all finished."

I looked at my two sisters to gauge their reaction. They were smiling. *This is great!* I decided. Our parents were getting along again. They must be, because they were cooperating on this. This also meant I'd see my friends in Burney. I hoped we could stay a long time. Maybe when Dad came to get us he'd decide never to go back to Utah!

The next Saturday we got up early for the ride to Bryce Canyon, the nearest town, where we would catch a bus. Dad drove us there in our new yellow 1961 Dodge Dart. It was sleek and could go really fast. At the bus station we had ice cream, then it was time for us to leave. I turned to Dad, who was hugging my sisters goodbye.

"See ya soon, Dad."

"Sure, Jim, have a good time," he said, squeezing me too tightly.

As the bus pulled away, I waved at him. He looked so masculine and strong standing on the curb with his broad shoulders and thick biceps. It felt kind of scary going back without him. Of course, we'd see him again soon, I assured myself. We'd all be back together. I held on to that idea as our bus passed through the canyons and into the flat deserts of Nevada. Hours passed, and finally I couldn't restrain myself any longer.

"Mom, how long before Dad comes and gets us?"

She turned to me and I saw the tears again. "Jimmy, your dad is never going to come for us. He doesn't want us anymore. He's found another family."

This time I believed her. The nightmare hadn't passed after all. I remembered Dad waving goodbye, standing there as we drove off. And then I remembered something else. Tall, strong Lucille. I thought of those times I had tried not to notice when she and Dad were talking and laughing, and all the times he'd been over at her trailer instead of ours. A dull ache filled my chest. The rest of the trip passed in a haze.

♪ ♪ ♪ ♪

As soon as we got back to Burney, we visited our old neighborhood. While Mom was with a friend, I slipped outside and went to a tall pine tree where my friends and I had carved our initials during happier days. I traced my fingers over the scars and remembered the way things used to be. I pressed my cheek to the rough bark and hugged the tree, holding on as tightly as I could. Would anything in my life ever be strong and secure again?

Mom enrolled at Chico State College. She was going back to school to become a teacher. Because we had no money, she and my sisters moved into a travel trailer in Chico, and I stayed in Burney with Dad's parents—two and a half hours away from Mom and my sisters.

Before going to Chico my mom took me to see my old friend, the foot doctor. I had been born clubfooted and had had surgery twice, once as a baby and again at the age of four. From then on I thought my feet were okay because I could outrun any of my classmates. Now, though, the doctor said he would have to operate one more time as soon as I got out of school.

I never thought I'd dread the beginning of summer vacation, but I did that year. When the day finally arrived, I sat dejectedly by Mom's side for the fifty-mile drive from Burney to Redding. Mom held my hand as we walked into the lobby, our footsteps echoing. The place smelled like medicine, and nurses scurried around on squishy, rubber-soled shoes. My mood improved when we got my room assignment. The kids' wing of the hospital was full, so I was going to be with the grown-ups. That made me feel important.

Soon it was time for Mom to go. She waved goodbye, looking terribly sad, and left me alone on the crisp, white bed. This was going to be a great adventure, I decided. Then a nurse came in and gave me an enema. What an indignity! *Nothing could be worse than this*, I thought, *not even surgery.* I was wrong, of course.

I was supposed to have bone fusion in both my feet. I didn't know what that meant, and no one had time to answer all the questions I had. They did tell me it was to stop my feet from growing. Without it, they said my feet would get worse as I got older. That explanation— when it was finally offered— helped a little, but I still got pretty irritated when I asked what anesthesia they were going to use and they told me "fairy dust." Oh, brother!

⬬ ⬬ ⬬ ⬬

When are they going to take me to surgery? I wondered as I woke up. Then all of a sudden I felt the pain. It was as though somebody had crushed my right foot. My whole leg throbbed, and I gritted my teeth. When Mom came, I begged for something to lessen the pain, but the nurses said no. I squirmed about, trying to find a position to ease the fire in my foot. But the pain wouldn't stop.

The doctor came in and explained that he hadn't been able to do both feet at once. I would have to be operated on again in ten days. A few days later, my foot began to itch under the cast. I pushed on the plaster until I made a hole, then I put my finger in to scratch. I touched something cold and hard. Strange vibrations spread down the middle of my foot. What was it? I pulled away the cotton and saw a steel spike sticking out of my foot!

I demanded answers from every person I saw. Finally they told me they had left steel pins in my foot until the bones could heal a little. Unfortunately, soon after the pain eased, the doctor scheduled surgery for my left foot. Once again I was back to sleepless nights. Only this time I was worn out and tired of the endless pain. I begged for a sleeping pill and finally got one. It felt so good to slip into a deep sleep.

In the middle of the night I woke up needing to go to the bathroom. When I tried to get up, I found bars on the sides of my bed. Undaunted, I crawled to the end of the bed and vaulted out—right onto the pins that protruded from the bottom of both my heels. I writhed on the floor, clenching my teeth and trying not to make any noise. The nurses had warned me never to bother my roommate—an elderly man. Finally I crawled around the bed and pushed the button to call the nurses. From then on, the nurse on the night shift tethered me to the bed when the lights went out.

After a month I was released from the hospital, but I was confined to a wheelchair for another six weeks. When I finally graduated to crutches, my legs felt like rubber, and my sense of balance was completely gone. I had to learn how to walk all over again. One day, after getting a new cast on my feet, I was told not to walk for several hours. When we arrived home, Mom had to pick me up like a 150-pound baby and lug me into the house. I could see her wince from the pain of my weight. I knew she had bursitis in her shoulder, and carrying me was making it worse. Squeezing my eyes shut against the sight, I decided never to be a burden again. I would get better, and I would never bother anyone again!

By the time school started I was getting around pretty well on my crutches. I hated myself for my handicap. I had gained too much weight during all the time in the hospital. I couldn't run and play like other kids, and my self-confidence had dipped to a new low. Why would anyone want to be around me? My own dad didn't even care about me!

Finally the doctor took the casts off for the last time. I thought I would be able to run and play immediately, but I faced another month of hobbling around. Even after months of recovery I had a strange, stiff gait. A few minutes on my feet and I would be in pain. Bullies at school began to make fun of the way I walked. Finally I picked one of the toughest and fought him. After that, the others left me alone.

Mom got a slightly larger place, and I moved in with her and my sisters again. Our house felt like an oven that August and September. Many times I lay sweating on the bed and wondered, *Is this all that life is? Why is it so hard? What's the point?* I spent more and more time in my room reading books. I didn't have many friends. As the months went by, my resentment toward my father grew. I thought about him and Lucille. Where were they? Didn't he even care about us? Did he know about my surgery?

We attended an ivy-covered church next to Chico State College. It seemed to help Mom, but it did nothing to ease the emptiness I felt inside. However, one special Sunday stands out in my memory. I was pretty nervous that morning because our confirmation class was to participate in the worship service, and I had a speaking part. As we kids filed past the white columns in the front pew, sunlight streamed through the windows, showing tiny dust motes swirling in front of the altar. Then the organ swelled into the opening anthem. I turned around to see several hundred people behind me on the pews. I gulped for air. Could I go through with it?

The hymns were sung and the Scriptures were read. *If only someone else could do my part*, I thought. I felt fat and incompetent, and wished I could walk better. Then, all too soon, the pastor was saying, "And now the confirmation class is going to do a special program for us."

We climbed to the stage, and when it was my turn, I limped to the pulpit, trying to remember my lines. I wondered if my voice would work at all. I looked out at the crowd. There was Mom, smiling at me.

"My people, the people of Israel…," I began. The words came out easily, and we made it through our whole program without any major disasters. Then it was over, and we made our way back to the pew. What a relief!

Mom was waiting at the door afterward. She hugged me. "Jim, you did a great job!" What else could a mom say? But then she added something very surprising. "You know, Jim, I think maybe you might be a minister someday."

TWO

A Heavenly Father

YEARS passed before my life became more than an exercise in stumbling along. Somehow Mom, my sisters, and I survived. Mom finished her master's degree and became a schoolteacher. I began to show more and more aptitude in school and even made a few friends. It was through one of those friends—a guy named Dan— that my faith in God really took hold and started to grow.

By this time I was ready to enter my sophomore year in high school. Dan and I had been working together on a ranch doing odd jobs. The work was hard but I liked it, and I enjoyed spending time with Dan and his family. They attended an Assembly of God church but usually called themselves Pentecostals. I didn't know what that meant, but something about the group appealed to me. Then Dan invited me to attend a camp meeting. Everyone was excited about it, and although I had no idea what I was in for, I accepted Dan's invitation. What did I have to lose?

The services were held in a big barn made of rough boards silvered with age. It seated about one thousand people and was full each night. The meetings certainly weren't like the services in our little ivy-covered church in Chico! People sang very loud, and when the preacher announced a time of prayer, I was shocked that everyone started praying out loud and raising their hands in the air. I felt awkward in such strange surroundings, but I couldn't deny the love I felt whenever I was around Dan's family and the others in their church. So, I kept going to the camp meetings. On the fifth night it happened.

I was sitting next to Dan on a hard-backed bench, my feet throbbing with pain from our long day of work. The preacher finished his message and made his usual appeal for non-Christians to come forward and "accept Jesus."

That seemed like an odd choice of words to me. Accept Jesus? I wondered if anybody there wasn't a Christian. I certainly was. I had always gone to church, and my family were good people.

The preacher was insistent: "Anyone who has business with God, come forward now." As the organ played softly, some people walked down the aisle. *Maybe I'd better go and do this*, I thought. I couldn't remember the last time I had talked to God.

"We're going to close the altar," the preacher said. "Any Christians who would like to come pray are welcome."

I was seated closest to the aisle, and Dan nudged me in an effort to get past. I stepped aside to let him out, then before I thought much about it, I followed him to the front. They ushered us into a room behind the speaking platform. Narrow straw kneeling mattresses were laid around the periphery of the room. I followed everyone else's example and knelt on one, facing the wall.

From that point, I didn't know what to do. People were crying and shouting all around me. The air was full of the smell of dust and straw. Right in front of my nose was a tiny spider in its web; I watched it for a few moments. Though I felt a little embarrassed, I had too much respect for God to get up and leave without saying anything. But what should I say?

I started thinking about Dan, his family, and the people in their church. They had something different and special. What caused that? Finally I mumbled, "God, I don't know what it is these people have, but they really love each other. I want that in my life. Can You give me whatever it is that makes them love each other like that, God?"

Suddenly something came crashing into my soul. I started trembling and burst into tears. It was wonderful and frightening—surely the best feeling I'd ever had. A power was taking over, and I didn't want it to stop. I don't know how long I stayed on my knees, but when I stood up the world seemed different. Everyone looked so good. Colors were more beautiful, smells more penetrating. Life suddenly took on new meaning, even if I didn't know what that meaning was.

*Ð. *Ð. *Ð. *Ð.

It didn't go away. Jesus was in my heart now, although I didn't understand much beyond that fact. My mom and sisters were puzzled at first, but shortly afterward all three of them were "born again." I hadn't seen my dad since that day he put us on the bus in Utah so many years ago, but now that I'd come to know my heavenly Father, I dared to hope I'd see my earthly dad again…someday.

My junior and senior years of high school hurried by; I felt as if I was at the beginning of a great adventure. Graduation was approaching, and I needed to make some decisions. One day I was riding with our pastor's son and asked him if he was going to be a preacher.

"No," he said, "I can't see myself as a pastor, but I could see you doing it." My mind went back to the words my mother had spoken in that ivy-covered church in Chico. Was that my calling? I never had a clear answer when I asked God what He wanted me to do, but slowly I put the clues together and began to believe He wanted me to be a missionary. Every time I heard a missionary speak at church something in me responded with excitement.

As I dared to earnestly think about a career in the mission field, I also began to consider all the obstacles in my way. Money topped the list. I'd have to study at Bethany Bible College, an Assemblies of God school that was very expensive. Although I couldn't afford tuition, somehow I knew I had to pursue my dream. I sent off for applications.

When the forms arrived they were easy to fill out, except for the part that asked how I was going to finance my education. I was more determined than ever to do what God was asking of me. I applied for scholarships and waited.

One day a letter came from the state of California. "Congratulations!" it began. I had been chosen as a state scholar, and all my tuition would be paid at any accredited university or college in California. A few days later another letter came. This one, from the federal government, informed me of a grant that was available to help with my studies. Now I not only had my tuition, but also a good part of my other expenses. The barriers were falling, and as far as I was concerned, I was on my way.

Then our senior-class counselor called me into his office. He was a large man who always wore a rumpled suit. He beamed as he moved aside piles of papers and beckoned me to sit down. He wasted few words in getting to the point.

"Jim, what are you going to do after high school?" he asked flatly.

"I'm going to Bethany Bible College to prepare for life as a missionary," I replied. I wasn't used to being public about my faith and felt a little embarrassed.

"What?" His smile was replaced by a look of incredulity. "You're a state scholar! You have money to study whatever you want, wherever you want. Are you going to throw all that away to be a…a *missionary*?"

I felt intimidated, but I wasn't going to back down now. "Yes, sir" was all I could come up with.

He fixed his eyes on mine. "Jim, I've never seen science and math scores like yours. You can write your own ticket. Some of the best universities in the world are here in California, and you can attend any one of them. Why would you choose a *Bible college*?"

The words *Bible college* sounded dirty and pitiful the way he said them. I wanted to tell him that this was God's call, not mine. "I just do," I said simply.

He kept shaking his head in disbelief. "Well, I don't know what to say. You can leave now, but I'll want to talk to you later."

I got up and fled, feeling like a prisoner set free, or at least an ex-prisoner on parole for a while. A few weeks later he called me back into his office and tried a different tactic.

"Jim, do you know there are Christians who believe no one should make his living from the ministry?" he asked.

He didn't wait for an answer. "The Bible itself says," he looked down at some notes, "to make it your ambition to lead a quiet life, to mind your own business, and to work with your hands, just as we have told you, so that your daily life may win the respect of outsiders and so that you will not be dependent on anybody." He looked at me and waited. I didn't know how to respond.

"You believe in the Bible, don't you, Jim? Maybe you should get yourself a real career. You can still do a lot for God, but you won't be dependent on others. What do you say?" He smiled expectantly.

His words confused me. What he had said was from the Bible, yet I couldn't deny the conviction that I was supposed to be a missionary. "I'm going to Bible college to become a missionary," I said, not looking him in the eye.

"Jim, you could be a research scientist. I've never seen a profile so suited to it. Please don't be stubborn." He was losing patience with me.

"I'm going to Bible college to become a missionary." By now the sentence was sounding like a chant. I knew I should have defended God's call to me, but the words wouldn't come. What kind of missionary was I going to be? At least I could be stubborn and stick to a purpose, but would that be enough?

❦❦❦❦

My decision proved to be a wise one. The first two years at Bethany Bible College went well. I became involved with a group of students who had been on summer outreaches with Youth With A Mission, or YWAM, as they called the organization. They were full of stories about ministry in the Caribbean and other places. I liked their faith and enthusiasm, and even though I found it difficult to do, I was soon spending most of my weekends going door-to-door witnessing with them.

I attended a house meeting where Loren Cunningham, the founder of YWAM, spoke. I was impressed. He actually believed we could reach the whole world. Loren encouraged us to do whatever God told us to do, no matter how impossible it seemed.

I wondered what it would be like to work in YWAM. Then I dismissed the idea and reminded myself that my future was with the Assemblies of God. I had even been chosen as a missionary intern to go to Guadalajara, Mexico, the next summer. Everything was falling into place. Or so I thought.

About that time I began to date a pretty classmate who also was training for missionary work. Her name was Dee Ann, and she made no secret about the fact that she had marriage on her mind. This was my first serious relationship, and I was unprepared for its rapid advancement from friendship to romance to engagement. My insecurity surfaced when she started talking about setting a wedding date. Intuition told me not to hurry, that we hadn't known each other very long, that we had two years of schooling left.

At the same time, I was afraid that if I didn't agree to her plans, she would lose interest in me. I wasn't exactly the best-looking guy on campus, and I was convinced she could do better.

At her insistence we first agreed on a late August wedding date that coincided with my return from the missionary internship in Mexico. But then Dee Ann announced that she didn't even want to wait that long. Our wedding was pushed up to early June, right after final exams. We had five days together before I left for my field assignment and Dee Ann began a summer job.

Our marriage was a terrible mistake, or so Dee Ann told me the evening I arrived home from Mexico. This was certainly not the kind of welcome I had expected! She blurted out that in my absence she had become involved with her supervisor at work—a married man with a family. Crushed by the news, I talked her into marriage counseling. She agreed, but the sessions had no long-term impact. She reluctantly accepted the counselor's suggestion of a reconciliation, but from that point on, our marriage was a series of make-up-break-up traumas. She left me twice during my senior year. Her final farewell took the form of a note, pinned to my pillow, that explained she had moved out to explore a "new relationship."

The whole situation was devastating to me. I believed then, as I believe now, that marriage is a lifelong commitment. However, no mutual consent is needed for divorce in California. Dee Ann was determined, and I had to accept the fact that our stormy marriage was over. I assumed all blame. I had failed.

~ ~ ~ ~

Somehow I made it through the final weeks of classes. All the while I felt as though I was living a charade—attending Bible college and going through a divorce. To make matters worse, our marriage wasn't the only part of my life that was in chaos. As my relationship with Dee Ann suffered, so did my commitment to God. I began hanging around with students who also were going through personal struggles. When some of the guys started experimenting with drugs, I tried marijuana. Maybe it would dull the pain, I decided.

Following graduation I took a part-time job. My life had no direction. The only thing I knew for sure was that I didn't want anything to do with religion, church, or Christians. Then one day I was playing chess with a guy who lived next door. He was smoking a joint, and I took a puff or two to be friendly. We were listening to the news on television, and a report came on about the "Jesus People."

"Those Christians are so false," I said.

He looked at me and one eyebrow shot up in surprise. "What do you mean? You're one of them."

I laughed out loud. "You've gotta be kidding. Here we are smoking dope and you think I'm a Christian?"

"You believe in Jesus, don't you?"

I opened my mouth to deny it, but the words just wouldn't come out. I was surprised. I couldn't deny Jesus! After all, He wasn't the one who had ruined my life. I went back to my room and collapsed on my bed, praying for the first time in months. "Lord, this is so stupid. How could I try and run away from You? I've messed up my whole life. I'm sorry for blaming You. I can't live away from You anymore. I don't know what I'm going to do, but I'm Yours, if You still want me."

Nothing in my circumstances had changed, but a spark of joy was reignited inside me. Jesus was back. I was still confused, but He was back.

Over the next couple of weeks I started to think about my future. I considered going to graduate school and pursuing some profession. But my calling wouldn't go away, even though it seemed impossible to fulfill. My denomination wouldn't accept me for the ministry because I was divorced. *Maybe I can go to graduate school and find acceptance in some other denomination*, I thought.

One bright summer morning I was sitting on the couch in my friend's house with a colorful clutter of graduate-school catalogs around me. The more I read, the more depressed and confused I got. This just didn't feel right, so I closed my eyes and prayed.

"Father, what do I do? I can't seem to get any idea of what You expect of me. What's my next step?"

I prayed for some time, then started to remember the challenge and faith of Loren Cunningham, the youthful founder of Youth With A Mission whom I had met during my sophomore year. I remembered the enthusiasm of those in YWAM. I wondered if their mission would accept someone who had messed up as badly as I had. As the morning wore on, I gradually came to the conviction that I should try to contact them. YWAM had an office somewhere in Southern California, and I thought I remembered the town. I called directory assistance and was rewarded with the number.

Within three weeks I had quit my job, sold my car, and was on my way to three months of classroom training followed by a three-month mission trip. It was sudden, but I had a strong feeling that I was on the right track. As I set off for Southern California, I was acutely aware that I was embarking on a new beginning. It was great to be on the move for God again, but at the same time, I felt a little apprehensive. Could someone with a life as scarred as mine really be used by God?

THREE

God's Answer

I ARRIVED in Sunland, a somewhat dilapidated suburb of Los Angeles, on a hot August day in 1972. The YWAM center— two houses sitting side by side—faced a big, dusty parking area. I took a deep breath, and it rasped in my throat. Looking around in disgust, I saw a brown pall over what appeared to be mountains in the background. How I missed the clean air of Northern California!

Someone showed me my room and I chose a bottom bunk, unpacked, and stretched out. I stared at the mattress above me, thinking, *This is home...at least for three months, then the mission trip.* After that, I wasn't sure, but I felt good. I had taken the step God wanted me to take. The rest was now up to Him.

I loved the Discipleship Training School. We had times of individual devotions, followed by intercessory prayer in small groups, then classroom study. Different instructors taught us each week. I had never heard teaching so aimed at changing the way a person lived.

Every class was focused on our walk with God. Every class seemed aimed directly at me.

We also had worship periods. I felt so good being back with the Lord. My conscience was becoming keener, and I was experiencing the inner voice of God, reading my Bible, and learning to pray by praying. We also had a good tape library that I used constantly.

What I needed now was a place to be alone with God and process my feelings and all the new things I'd learned. Solitude was at a premium with forty people crammed into two houses. I took over a walk-in closet that wasn't being used because the clothes rod was missing. I "furnished" it with a chair and a quilt. It was small and cramped, but during free time I would go there with teaching tapes and my Bible.

One day I listened to a tape by Joy Dawson on the subject of spiritual brokenness. She explained how we need God to show us the wrongs in our heart. I switched off the tape recorder and stretched out the length of the closet. I closed my eyes. "Father, is there anything in my heart that doesn't please You?" I waited, pretty sure God would find nothing wrong. After all, I was spending my free time in a closet praying. I was surprised when the thought came into my mind. *Yes, there is. You have never forgiven your father.*

"But, Lord, that was years ago. It doesn't bother me."

It bothers you more than you know. And even if it didn't affect you, it is unacceptable to Me.

"But I never even think about it anymore."

It's there, the presence seemed to say, *and you have to let go of it.*

I finally prayed, "Okay, Lord. I forgive my dad...." The tears started running down my cheeks as I remembered. I recalled saying goodbye to Dad and getting on the bus. He said he'd see us in California. Then I remembered my mom struggling to carry me into the house after my surgery. Then there was the cramped apartment and the hard times. I remembered it all.

"Lord, I do forgive my dad. I forgive him. I forgive Lucille, too. Help me to forgive them." It was like a dam had broken. I cried and cried, and felt the pain ease. Until that moment I didn't realize how much my attitude toward my dad had poisoned me. When I finished praying, though, my attitude had changed so drastically that it stunned me. I had been living a true experience with Jesus, but only now did I feel free and clean inside.

Three months later I received word from a Christian uncle that my father had given his life to Jesus! I was convinced the timing was no coincidence.

                                               ~ ~ ~ ~

When our classroom training was over, we went on a mission trip to Hawaii. As much as I anticipated ministering in one of the most exotic destinations on earth, I never guessed the wonders that Hawaii had in store for me.

We were met at the airport by the junior leader of our school, a fun-loving and articulate young man named John Dawson. He divided us into small teams, and we spread out all over the island of Oahu for evangelism. Two months of ministry followed. Nothing major happened, not until we came to the town of Kailua on the windward side of Oahu. We were to give a training course at a church and stay in a house next door.

One day I saw a young woman on the porch of our house. Her long, brown hair had been bleached by the Hawaiian sun, and she wore a long, flowing dress. She was crouched down helping someone with guitar chords. When I passed, something jumped inside me. I asked around and learned her name was Pam Medeiros. Everyone admired her commitment to God.

The first time I talked with Pam I noticed her brown eyes. They could be very intense when something important held her attention. As the days passed I found myself hoping someday her eyes would focus on me with that intensity.

In subsequent weeks, Pam filled more and more of my thoughts. She came to hear me teach every night in the church. I decided this was a sure sign of her spiritual hunger…and her good taste. I found myself watching as she worshiped the Lord in the meetings. I found it difficult to close my eyes; I only wanted to look at her. I learned she was called to the mission field, too, and was studying nursing at the University of Hawaii.

I think what drew me most was Pam's strength and serenity. Here was a girl who was real and who probably wouldn't melt at the first sign of difficulties. Of course, there was also her smile, and the way her mouth turned down slightly at the corners. That smile haunted my thoughts.

One day I walked Pam to her car. We leaned against it while she told me how she had come to know the Lord. Her family was part of the Portuguese community in Hawaii—in fact, her dad was a state representative. They were strong Catholics. However, she hadn't found spiritual reality in that church. Then, during high school, she had taken a temporary job at a circus. A Brazilian man worked at a booth near hers. Before returning to Brazil, he sat down with her, explained the gospel, then led her in the sinner's prayer.

She eventually found her way to the church where we met. I thought, *How interesting that God would use a man from Brazil to lead an American girl in Honolulu to Jesus.*

I told Pam a little of my story and about the divorce. I was afraid that would discourage our friendship. I was relieved when she smiled and said I should leave that in the past and get on with my life.

When the day came to leave Hawaii, I walked into the large, cool concrete airport and smiled. There was Pam sitting in a black chair bent over something. I walked up and found she was working intently with a needle on what looked like a cloth cover for a Bible. "Here, Jim. I made this for you." She handed it to me. The words from the first chapter of Joshua were embroidered on it in bold colors: "Be strong and courageous! Do not tremble or be dismayed, for the Lord your God is with you wherever you go."

I carefully wrapped my Bible in its new handmade cover and tucked it into my satchel. The fact that she had taken time to make the cover seemed encouraging. Could she be interested in a penniless, chubby missionary who waddled slightly when he walked?

Back in Southern California I wrote and thanked Pam for the Bible cover. She responded by thanking me for thanking her. I replied, thanking her for her gracious acknowledgment of my gratitude. We were writing!

As the months passed, our relationship moved from interesting to serious—at least for me. For a year we traded letters. Following the training school, I joined a YWAM evangelism team and had adventures in Russia and Mexico. It was a great year, but the most significant aspect of it was the correspondence with Pam.

I was careful in my letters to say nothing about romantic love. I had learned more about love during my training with YWAM—things I wished I had known earlier. Now I understood love was a commitment of heart, not a state of emotions. I wouldn't tell Pam I loved her to get the emotional kick that can come from such a declaration. This was either of God or it wasn't, but I had to do it right this time.

My greatest problem was I wanted Pam so much. Was God leading me, or was I being led astray by desire again? I didn't believe anyone should ever divorce, but it had happened to me. Could God forgive me and give me a new life? Everything I knew about Him indicated that He would, but I wanted to be sure.

I had some vacation time coming, so two friends and I headed for the Olympic Mountains in Washington state. We spent three weeks trout fishing and mountain climbing. We were surrounded by crystalline lakes and streams, evergreen forests, and snow-covered peaks. And we had a lot of time to pray.

One day it started to snow. Without any wind, the flakes drifted down in slow motion. I hiked to a nearby lake, found a rocky point, and stood there. I watched the snow silently carpet the lake and mountains. I almost ached with the beauty of it as the quiet seeped into me. The presence of God was strong. While standing silently in the snow, I became convinced of two things: First, I would marry Pam; and second, we would serve the Lord somewhere in Latin America.

During the next several days I struggled with those two ideas. I desperately wanted to marry Pam, but I was afraid it was my idea, not God's. And the part about Latin America was disappointing. I wanted to go to the Muslim world, or Asia, or the Communist Bloc. Something big and important. Latin America seemed tame and insipid. I wanted something harder. But the more I prayed, the more I was convinced that God wanted Pam and me in Latin America.

When I returned from vacation I wondered what my next step should be. I needed to go to Hawaii and spend time with Pam. What if she wasn't feeling the same things I was? Since I had been working without salary as a YWAM volunteer, I didn't have even $10 in my pocket. I knelt one day to pray, asking God for my next step in ministry...and, of course, about Pam. The floor was hard in the dorm house, so I found an old throw rug and doubled it a few times to put beneath my knees. I picked up my Bible with the embroidered cover that Pam had made and laid it open in front of me. I was going to stay a while.

An hour later I was still praying. "Father, what do I do now? It seems my leaders have no new projects for me. Where do You want me to go? What do You want me to do?" Pam was never far from my thoughts, and now on my knees I remembered the strong impressions I had received in the mountains as the snow fell that day. Just then the phone rang. It was a friend from the Bay Area, asking if I knew any YWAMers who could work for two weeks.

"Sorry, I don't know of anybody," I said, glad when the phone call was over so I could go back to praying. I had to hear from God, and such interruptions didn't help. No sooner had I gotten settled back onto my folded rug than a thought came into my mind: *Jim, that call was a sign from me. That's your next step. You take that job and earn the money for your ticket to Hawaii. I want you to go.*

I called my friend, took the temporary job, and two weeks later left for Honolulu.

Pam was the only one who knew I was coming. She was supposed to meet me at the airport, and the anticipation inside me was running high. That was the longest flight of my life. I read, watched some of the movie, relocated to the other part of the giant 747, and watched another movie. I counted and recounted the passengers on the almost-empty jumbo jet. Nothing came close to calming me. My whole future hinged on the next few hours. Would I get it right? Was I really hearing from God? Was this wonderful girl going to be my wife? Did she feel the way I did, or would I make a fool of myself? Could God really wipe out my past and give me a new start?

Finally we landed. It was early afternoon. The air was warm, humid, and vaguely exotic. I pushed through the wood and glass doors to the sidewalk where I would catch a little shuttle into the main terminal area. I heard a voice to my left.

"Jim!"

I turned and saw Pam. She was dressed in a floor-length print cotton dress and sandals. The breeze caught her brown glossy hair. In her hands was a white flower lei. I caught my breath.

FOUR

Steps of Faith

S H E looked as shy as I felt. I decided she looked like she needed help, so I walked over and lowered my head a bit. She slipped the flowers around my neck, and we gave each other a self-conscious hug.

"Good flight?" she asked.

"Yeah, it was fine." Conversation wasn't exactly flowing, but the way I felt, who cared? We made our way out through baggage claim and got into her little white Toyota. She had left the rest of her day free, so we decided to drive around the island. As we passed tall green peaks, fields of pineapple, and palm-fringed beaches, we talked about each other's calling, experiences with God, our hopes, and our dreams. At sundown she pulled the car over at a park.

We walked under high, stately palms out to where the white sand swept down into the intense blue water of the Pacific. We sat on a bench. Two boats glided by, their canvas sails tinted with the colors of the sunset. A light breeze bathed us in gentle warmth. I had to tell her my feelings.

I turned and started to open my mouth, but nothing came out. I was determined not to mention love until I had made a commitment. But I'd never told her my feelings and didn't know if I could run the risk. *Jim*, I thought, *this is ridiculous! You've been praying about this for months. There will never be a better time.*

"Pam, I love you."

I held my breath and waited for her response. She looked at me with what looked like utter serenity. She smiled and said, "I love you, too."

We smiled some more and then went back to watching the sunset. I didn't know what else to say. When the pink and gold finally faded from the sky, we got back in the car and drove to the bluff overlooking moonlit Hanauma Bay. We got out and sat on a low lava wall and talked into the evening. I wasn't sure what she meant by saying she loved me—loved me as a brother? as a friend?—but my declaration was permanent.

"Pam, I've prayed a lot, and I believe God wants us to be together. We're both called to be missionaries in Latin America."

This isn't supposed to be a business proposition, Jim! I reminded myself. I tried a different tack.

"I...uh...what I mean to say is, I don't want to go to South America without you. You're the best thing in my life since I found Jesus, and I don't want to lose you, Pam. Will you marry me?"

"Maybe."

My heart fell. "Maybe? What do you mean maybe?"

She looked away, drawing her knees up and wrapping her arms around them. Finally she turned to me, smiling that wonderful smile. "I mean, yes." I leaned over and kissed her. I'd never been so happy in my life.

❧ ❧ ❧ ❧

We now faced another challenge. Even though Pam and I were both of age, we wanted her parents' blessing. This wouldn't be easy, since our plans to go to South America sounded unrealistic even to me. Finally, we asked her parents if we could talk to them, and they agreed. Pam picked me up where I was staying with Christian friends, and we drove over to their comfortable neighborhood.

My heart was thudding loudly enough to be heard on the next block. I knew Pam had been raised in very prosperous circumstances and had attended the most exclusive high school in Hawaii, commuting in her own car. Her dad was a state legislator, a man of distinction on the islands. And here I was, a penniless missionary candidate headed vaguely to somewhere in Latin America.

As we walked up the curved driveway past the neat Japanese garden with its big boulders, I was starting to get nervous. We came to the side door where several pairs of shoes were neatly lined up. Everyone in Hawaii is expected to take off his shoes before entering a home. I stooped down and untied my laces. Without my shoes I would have trouble walking, and my limp would be more noticeable. When we entered the kitchen, I was surprised. It was the first I had seen with carpeting. There was even a color television to watch while cooking.

"Hi, honey," Pam's mom said, greeting her with a kiss. "Hello, Jim, how are you?" She looked cool despite the heat outside.

I struggled to get my words organized in my head as we made our way into the formal living room. We passed dark Oriental furniture beside a long glass wall that opened onto the pool surrounded by a profusion of tropical plants. Pam's dad joined us in the living room. He projected power even in an open-collared shirt.

"Hello, Jim. Hi, Pammie." He gave Pam a peck on the cheek and sat beside his wife on the white sofa. Pam and I sat down cross-legged on the carpet and made self-conscious small talk. Then everyone was silent. It was my turn.

"Uh, Mr. and Mrs. Medeiros...Pam and I have been talking...." I didn't look at Pam, but I could feel her calm presence beside me. "I...uh, that is, we...we want to get married."

I waited, then added, "We want to ask your blessing. That's very important to us."

Pam's mother looked at her husband, then asked me, "Where will you live?"

I knew the questions behind the question. What about your financial situation? How will you support our daughter?

"We both believe we're supposed to be missionaries in Latin America." The words sounded thin and the dream incredible sitting there in the elegant living room. "We won't set up permanent house-keeping until we're down there."

Finally Mr. Medeiros spoke up. "Don't you think you ought to get more established before you consider such a serious step as marriage?"

I glanced at Pam. "Well, we've spent a lot of time considering this. There's no way to get established before we actually go. And we want to be married before we leave."

I was holding my breath, hoping he wouldn't ask anything more specific...like how was I going to pay for the trip down, or what we would live on when we got there. I didn't want to tell this prestigious man that we were going to trust God!

"Of course, if you don't agree, we won't get married," I offered.

"Oh no, we wouldn't stand in the way," he replied.

I smiled and looked at Pam as we stood up. "Well, at least we have that over with!" I said. Everyone laughed.

❧ ❧ ❧ ❧

We were married on April 6, 1974, the day after I turned twenty-four. Pam was three years younger. Within a few months, she graduated with a nursing degree, and we attended another YWAM training course on the Big Island of Hawaii. It turned out to be important because we spent time with the directors of YWAM in Latin America, Wedge and Shirley Alman.

The Almans listened as we discussed our leading toward Latin America. YWAM wasn't a very large mission at that time, and from what I learned from Wedge and Shirley, it had barely gotten started in South America. The Almans had been in virtually all the countries with a team of volunteers. Now they were starting a permanent effort in Bogotá, Colombia. That left the rest of the continent open. All we had to learn was where Pam and I should go. I hoped we could hear clear direction from God.

We had expected to go to a Spanish-speaking country, but that began to change. Loren Cunningham mentioned Brazil several times in the classroom, and somehow it stayed in my heart. The more I prayed, the greater the idea grew. God wanted us to go to Brazil. Pam agreed. Later, we saw the signs that had been there all along: Pam was from a Portuguese family, and Brazilians speak Portuguese. She had even been won to the Lord by a Brazilian!

It was one thing to know God wanted us to go to Brazil; it was another to figure out how to get there. We still owed $1,000 on our training course in Hilo. We had no committed monthly support, and at that time YWAM workers weren't accustomed to going out and finding donors. All we could do was pray and wait for God to provide.

We didn't know anyone in Brazil. However, Rudy Lack, a YWAM leader from Switzerland, visited Hawaii en route to Brazil. He promised he'd try to prepare the way for us with Christians in Brazil.

Meanwhile, Pam and I thoroughly researched Brazil. We learned it was roughly the same size as the lower forty-eight states and had the largest population in all of South America. We pored over maps. Brazil sprawled over much of the continent, bordering every country except Ecuador and Chile. We traced the length of the Amazon River—four thousand miles across the continent—and tried to imagine the jungles, as well as the mountains and plains to the south.

I was fascinated to read of Brazil's people, perhaps the most racially mixed in the world, descending from Portuguese settlers, other Europeans, Arabs, Asians, native Indians, and Africans. It was the largest Roman Catholic country in the world, too. However, we also read about *macumba*, an Afro-Brazilian religion that many of the people practiced along with their Catholicism.

One night I lay in our apartment and thought about Brazil. Who were we to go into such a vast country and start a mission? What if we failed? While Pam slept beside me, I remembered the conversation with her parents and their unspoken question: How will you take care of our daughter? Here was this young woman from a prosperous family in Honolulu, and I was taking her into the unknown without an extra dollar in my jeans. I lay there in the dark trying to remember the messages on faith we had learned in our YWAM training.

꿈 꿈 꿈 꿈

On the final day of our training course, I went to the bookkeeper to give her our last ten dollars. We still owed $1,000. As I laid down the ten dollars, I said, "I don't know how we'll do it, but Pam and I will not go to Brazil until we pay all we owe the school."

The bookkeeper looked in her ledger and ran her finger down the list of figures. "No, Jim, you don't owe anything. It's been paid."

I stared for a second. I didn't want to ask what had happened. I was afraid the miracle would disappear. Finally I asked who had paid our bill. She wouldn't say. Our first problem was gone. Just like that!

It was almost Christmas, and Pam's folks had sent us tickets to Oahu so we could spend the holidays with them. Pam and I agreed to pray a lot about specific direction during the Christmas season. The more we prayed, the more we realized we were to leave for Brazil very soon, even though we had no money and still hadn't heard from Rudy Lack about any invitations from Brazilian churches or missions. We decided to go to South America one step at a time. First we'd spend some time with Mom in California. There was no telling when we'd be back in America again.

We closed the savings account that we had kept open with a symbolic amount after our wedding. That netted us $15. We had a few other small offerings come our way, but we were still about $225 dollars short for our tickets to California. Christmas fell on a Wednesday, and we made reservations for a flight out on Thursday morning,

December 26. That left seven days to raise the money. Six, really, since Wednesday would be a holiday.

On the Sunday before Christmas, I was to preach at our home church. Pam had gone there since she became a Christian. I'd been very active in the church during the months we were waiting to be married. Maybe they would give us an offering generous enough to cover our tickets. Maybe they'd decide to give regular donations—our projected monthly support was still zero.

I preached as well as I knew how, and the pastor approached me afterward. "Jim, I've talked it over with some of the elders, and we may want to support you and Pam on the field. Can you come back and preach again tonight? We can confirm your support then."

Can I! Our church was behind us. Surely they would give us an offering that night. Monthly support was important but not nearly as urgent as the $225 we needed to leave for the mainland in four days.

After I spoke that evening, the pastor came to me with a smile. "Jim, we're going to support you on the field," he said. "We were going to send $15 a month, but we really liked your ministry today, and we've decided to increase the amount to $50."

That was great news! But how could we catch the plane on Thursday? The pastor continued, "We usually give an offering to our guest speakers."

I held my breath.

"However, we don't do that for the speakers we regularly support."

Oh no! At this rate we'd never get off the island.

"In your case, we decided to make an exception. Here is a love offering." He handed me an envelope. It seemed like bad manners to look at the amount, so I slipped the envelope into my pocket and tried to pay attention to the rest of our conversation. As soon as I could, I excused myself and rushed outside. Standing under the light of a streetlamp, I ripped open the envelope. I read the numbers: $25. My excitement died. Only four days were left to come up with $200.

Family Ties

O N Christmas Eve I reminded God that if $200 in checks didn't arrive by the noon mail, we wouldn't have time to cash them. The banks would be closed. Noon came and went. The banks closed without a visit from us.

We gathered at Pam's parents' home for a family celebration. Although it was Christmas Eve, the weather was warm and the windows open. A tall fir tree decorated with red balls and multicolored lights stood in the living room. I looked halfheartedly at the elegantly wrapped gifts beneath the tree. All I could think was, *We're supposed to leave the day after tomorrow and we can't pay for our tickets.* Oh, how I hated to tell Pam's parents of our situation.

We sat down on the pale furniture, and I picked up my first present. It had a red bow and felt light. I opened it and discovered a $50 bill inside! Pam opened a similar package and found $50, too. I was encouraged. Of course, it didn't affect the outcome, I reminded myself.

Lacking $100 was as much an obstacle as lacking $200. And just as embarrassing. I picked up another package, trying to disguise the slight disappointment when it felt heavier. I opened the box and folded back the crisp white tissue lining. A shirt. And another $50! When Pam opened her next package, she found a robe and $50. Our eyes met and we grinned. We had exactly $200 in cash—no banks needed. That, added to the $25 from our church, was exactly the price of our tickets.

The day after Christmas we were on our way to Brazil, although we only had tickets as far as San Francisco. We spent the New Year's holiday with Mom and then headed south to stay temporarily at the same center where I had started out in YWAM, those two houses side by side in dusty Sunland, California.

Rudy Lack, our friend from Switzerland who had visited Brazil, wrote and sent the address of a group called Bethany Fellowship Missions, "Betânia" in Portuguese. The ministry was located in a city called Belo Horizonte. He said the members might be able to help us. Pam and I consulted our map. It was about 270 miles inland from Rio de Janeiro. We wrote and soon received a letter from a Betânia missionary, saying they had lined up a Brazilian family who would take us as boarders, and they had located a language teacher. The room and board would cost $70 a month, and the language study, $50 a month. I folded the letter and replaced it in its envelope. We could trust God for $70 above the $50 promised from our church in Hawaii. It would be hard but not impossible.

As shaky as these plans seemed, Pam and I felt we could leave soon, going through Colombia to spend a short time with Wedge and Shirley Alman. From there we would proceed to Brazil. I went to a nearby park and sat on a bench, praying about the timing of our departure from Sunland. To my surprise I began to think about my dad. I remembered him standing there as the Greyhound bus had pulled away, fourteen years ago. An idea began to take shape. We should go see Dad on our way to Brazil.

When I told Pam, she agreed with me. Dad and I had exchanged only a few letters, but I knew he lived near Phoenix. I got his number from directory assistance, then stood at the pay phone with his number in my hand. What would I say? I dropped in the coins and listened for the number to ring.

"Stier residence." The voice hadn't changed.

"Dad? It's Jim."

Silence. Finally, "Jim? Where are you? Is anything wrong?"

"No, Dad. Nothing wrong...." I paused. What do you say after fourteen years? "I just wanted to call and talk to you. I've...I've gotten married, Dad. Pam and I...that's her name...Pam...we are on our way to Brazil, and I wanted to see you before we left."

He didn't hesitate. "Why sure, Jim, we'd love to see you." At the sound of the word *we* I remembered Lucille, the tall, strong woman who had changed everything. I took a deep breath, remembering that I'd forgiven her as well. Then he told me something really surprising. His phone had been disconnected because of overuse by Lucille's teenaged daughters. "I just got the phone reconnected today," he explained. "In fact, the man left fifteen minutes ago from hooking it up again. Then you called!"

I didn't say anything, but I smiled. The Lord was in this. He would also help us put our relationship back together.

Pam and I got a ride with some YWAMers headed in that general direction. We found the neighborhood outside Phoenix, and finally, the address my dad had given me. It was quite a way out of town. A few houses were sprinkled over the barren desert. It looked a little like that bleak place in Utah where we had last lived together.

We arrived earlier than expected, and no one was home. Our friends were anxious to get back on the road, so we told them to go on. Their Volkswagen quickly disappeared down the sandy street, leaving Pam and me with our luggage, sleeping bags, and Pam's guitar. We sat down on Dad's porch and waited an hour until a battered white Dodge van lumbered down the street. My dad jumped out and came to meet us, walking a bit slower than I remembered. I still recognized him, although he had lost most of his athletic figure, and his hair had receded, making his widow's peak more pronounced.

"Dad...."

We hugged, and the years dropped away. It was as natural to hug him as it had been when I was a young boy. We went into the house and sat down to talk. We had no trouble finding things to discuss because now Dad was really excited about God. A couple of hours later, Lucille came home. She smiled uncertainly as she entered the room. I closed the distance between us and put my arms around her. Then I noticed a gangly teenaged boy coming in the door.

"Jim, you have a brother. This is Wesley. He's fourteen," Dad said. I hugged Wesley, too.

≈ ≈ ≈ ≈

We had a good visit with my dad, Lucille, Wesley, and Lucille's daughters. We caught up on a lot of lost years. However, the departure for South America was on our minds. We planned to leave in two weeks but still had no idea how we would get the $900 needed for our flights to Bogotá, Colombia, to see Wedge and Shirley, let alone the remainder to go from Colombia to Brazil. We were broke, and the prospects didn't look too bright. I told my father about our situation. Perhaps now that he was a Christian he would profit from seeing the miracle that I was convinced was going to happen. I tried not to think about how Dad would be affected by a miracle that didn't happen.

One day as we worked in his vegetable garden, he leaned on the handle of his spade and looked at me. "Jim, I heard a speaker once who had received a call to China. He said yes to God, and then the Lord told him he didn't have to go. It was enough that he was willing. Maybe something like that is happening with you now."

It was a tantalizing thought. We were only ten days from departure and still lacked most of the money. Hardly any potential donors knew where we were. It would have been such a relief to stop pushing and take a different, easier direction with our lives. Who could blame us? But that wouldn't be right. I would hold on to what we thought God had told us.

"No," I said and picked up my hoe again, attacking the hardened ground with new vigor. "God isn't like that, Dad. He wouldn't mislead us. If He told us we are going to Brazil, then that's where we're going."

Although I kept my eyes on my work, I could sense Dad's disbelief.

The miracle started to unfold the next day. Our mail was forwarded from California and Hawaii. First, I got back three years' of income tax refunds I didn't expect. Then a friend sent a check, and Dad and Lucille gave us their last $100. Many other things happened, and two days before our departure we had all but $20. Where would the last bit come from?

We had to pay for our tickets on Thursday, and on Wednesday night I spoke to a tiny group at the country church my dad and Lucille attended. When I finished, the congregation took up an offering: $23. My father was more impressed by that $23 offering than by anything else. He had never seen his church give anything to a guest speaker. To him, that was the real miracle.

On Thursday we went down and bought our tickets from Phoenix to Bogotá, with a return to Miami. Without a return ticket to the United States, we wouldn't be allowed into Colombia. Early Friday we went to the airport. Our baggage was overweight, and we didn't have the money to pay the excess. We opened our suitcases and began taking things out until our luggage was light enough. We said goodbye and left Dad and his family standing with a bundle of our clothes in their arms.

❧ ❧ ❧ ❧

We were met in cool, crisp Bogotá by Wedge and Shirley. They took us to the Bible school where they were conducting a short-term training school. We planned to stay two weeks before continuing to Brazil.

Everything seemed so foreign, especially the food. We ate typical Colombian food in a common dining room. One day I walked past the kitchen, and a strange odor wafted past. Was someone boiling cow manure? Nausea washed over me. Pam and I hadn't reacted well to the local water, and we both had suffered with bouts of dysentery. To my surprise, I found out they were cooking cow intestines with garbanzo beans!

When lunchtime came, we sat down resolutely in the dining room. I dipped my spoon into the smelly, soupy stuff and sipped it gingerly. I could feel the wiggly, wavy parts of the intestines that push the food along the cow's digestive system. I grabbed for my drink and gulped. It was sickly sweet. My tablemates explained it was *panela*, a drink made from boiling solid brown blocks of raw sugar. I felt a long way from home.

If getting used to the food was difficult, making friends with the Colombians was easy. Wedge and Shirley's students were intelligent, warm, and enthusiastic about God. One day they surprised us by taking up an offering for me to buy a suit. I was embarrassed by their generosity, but I also appreciated it. I went shopping and chose a dark blue suit, the first I had ever owned.

Meanwhile, our departure for Brazil was rushing upon us. I learned we could turn in our return tickets to Miami and apply the credit toward one-way tickets to Rio de Janeiro. Gratefully, Brazil did not require proof of return tickets for entry. But even if we did that, we would still be $500 short. The day before departure, Wedge and Shirley called us into their combination bedroom and office. "Let's pray and see if you are to go to Brazil at this time," Wedge said. It hit me then. Wedge and Shirley doubted whether or not we should be allowed to start YWAM in Brazil. I felt a twinge of alarm.

We prayed for several minutes and then quietly waited on the Lord to speak to our hearts. Wedge was at his desk with his Bible open, while Shirley sat on their bed with her eyes tightly closed. Pam bowed her head beside me, and I closed my eyes but couldn't concentrate. I heard Wedge rustling the pages of his Bible.

"Listen to this, guys," Wedge said. He looked thoughtful. "I got an impression to look up Joshua 10:22. Listen to what Joshua said: 'Open the mouth of the cave and bring those five kings out to me.' That's perfect." Then he looked at us. "Don't you get it?"

I groped for something to say, but the truth was, it meant absolutely nothing to me. Then Shirley said, "Let me see that!" Suddenly she started laughing. "Of course! Don't you see? Five kings!" she said.

No, I don't see, I thought.

"Five kings is the $500 you need to leave tomorrow. We're supposed to go into our 'cave' and bring out the five kings."

Cave?

"Wedge, I think we should take up an offering from our students. That's the cave where five kings are waiting for Jim and Pam." She smiled, and now Wedge was smiling, too, and agreeing.

Well, I thought, *that's an interesting exegesis of Scripture!* I bet my Bible college professors would find it unorthodox, to say the least. And surely this group of thirty Latin students didn't have $500 among them. As the four of us prayed again, though, we agreed perhaps this was what God was telling us to do.

Wedge announced our need the next day in class. He suggested another offering for us. I was embarrassed. They had already given such a generous amount for my suit. After they filed out to lunch, we sat down to count the wad of colored bills. I knew the Colombian peso was worth only a few cents in U.S. currency. Futility swept over me. We were counting pennies, and in only an hour or two at the most, we had to go downtown and buy $500 worth of tickets.

Just then Wedge was called out of the room. He came back with a smile. "Guess what, Jim! One of the students from Argentina has decided to give you her return ticket to Buenos Aires. With that we should have enough."

Wedge, Shirley, Pam, and I rushed into Bogotá to the Avianca Airlines office. We had learned a flight was leaving early the next morning but that we couldn't buy tickets at the airport. We had to get to the airline office before it closed. We dashed in the direction of Avianca and arrived just as a guard was closing the doors. We frantically explained our situation and he relented. We sat down with the only woman still on duty and explained what we wanted. She frowned.

"The ticket from Argentina can only be redeemed or transferred in Buenos Aires. I'm sorry, sir. We can't help."

I sat there stunned, then looked over at Pam. What were we going to do? Wedge excused himself and went to talk with Shirley in the corner. They came back and Wedge announced, "We believe God wants you in Brazil, and we are to do everything we can to help. Shirley and I have received a few donations during the past few days. We believe God will meet our needs some other way. There should be enough in our account to cover the rest of your tickets."

As I sat there speechless, Wedge wrote a check for the rest of our fare. We walked out with our tickets, happy, relieved, and at the same time humbled. What generosity from people who had so little themselves!

The next morning we arrived early at the airport. We always believed we had to pay our tithes, so I had given our last money to Wedge and Shirley in obedience to this principle. Once again we were checking in for an international flight with almost no money. This time our pocket change amounted to exactly three dollars. Just as we were about to board, Wedge came up and handed me a check for $60.

"We want you guys to have this," he said. "I only wish it were more."

SIX

Welcome to Brazil

T H E cabin lights brightened as the jet engines took on a higher pitch and our plane tilted downward for its descent into Rio de Janeiro. God had worked so many miracles to get us here. We had to trust Him now. I smiled to myself as we gathered our carry-on luggage. I felt a sense of permanency. After all, we were here on one-way tickets.

My good humor left me as we lined up for customs. Would the immigration officer ask how much money we had? Would he insist on seeing a return ticket after all? All too soon I was standing in front of him. He barely looked at us, took our new passports, and after the briefest glance, stamped them. Welcome to Brazil!

Our next challenge was to find a place to sleep. David Eby, the Betânia missionary, had sent the phone number of a friend in Rio who might give us lodging. Of course, since our money had come in at the last minute, I hadn't called ahead. I realized I had to find a place to change my three dollars into cruzeiros, then find a phone. Pam sank onto the suitcases to wait, looking as exhausted as I felt.

The man at the exchange window gave me a handful of unfamiliar bills and coins, which I spread out in front of him and pantomimed dialing a telephone. He started spouting Portuguese, finally indicating one of the coins. Just to be sure, I pantomimed putting that coin into a pay phone and dialing. He shook his finger back and forth in what I assumed was a "no." He burst into a long explanation, but I didn't understand a word.

I left the exchange window totally confused and followed the pictures of phones until I found a telecommunications office with a bank of telephone booths near a counter where people lined up to send telegrams. I went to one of the booths and tried to insert every coin I had. Nothing fit. Then I stretched up on tiptoe until I could see. The slot had grooves in it. Of course! The man had tried to tell me that I'd have to exchange a coin for a token!

I lined up at the counter and bought tokens and went to try again. Still, no luck. This time I got an unintelligible recording in Portuguese. Now I was getting irritated. I stared at the handful of tokens and the assorted change. What was I going to do? How could I make it in this country if I couldn't even make a phone call?

I sat down beside Pam on the other suitcase. We must have looked pretty forlorn because someone from the telecommunications office came and got my scrap of paper with the number scribbled on it and went to work for us. They chattered away in Portuguese, smiling, and dialing the number. Someone finally turned up who spoke a bit of English. He explained we had a wrong number, then somehow he got the right number, and the person was on the phone. I talked with a woman—an American, thank goodness. Her husband was away on a trip, but she and her sons would come after us.

We went into the terminal to wait. The doors were all open to the night, and the air was warm and balmy. It felt a lot like Hawaii. We watched people pass by as we waited. I noticed most Brazilians were very brown. Then the most stunningly beautiful woman I'd ever seen walked by. She was the color of coffee with cream and had long, glossy black hair. She was wearing a well-tailored green pantsuit. I tapped Pam and asked, "Did you see that woman?"

Pam pressed her lips tight and said, "Yes, and I think maybe we should go back to the States."

"Oh, I don't know. I'm starting to like the idea of living here."

We laughed and some of the tension faded. It was good to finally be in Brazil. It was good to have come to the place where God wanted us to stay. And it was wonderful to have Pam beside me. Perhaps it was just as well that we didn't know what all lay ahead. Our courage might have failed.

Just then a white Volkswagen van pulled up outside with three white faces peering anxiously toward us. We were soon on our way to a night of hospitality with a missionary family.

❧ ❧ ❧ ❧

We had bought our tickets through to Belo Horizonte from Bogotá, and the next day we were on a plane for the one-hour flight to the city that would be our new home. David Eby, the missionary from Betânia, and a friend met us at the airport. They were very friendly, and their welcome lowered my anxiety level quite a bit. Maybe they didn't see us as too much of a nuisance. They explained their center was quite close by, and off we went.

The traffic was wild. Our car ricocheted among the traffic. Lots of car horns blared, and drivers who could edge half a car length ahead cut in front of us. Again and again we escaped collision by inches. When I could tear my eyes away from the chaos, I noticed David was quite calm at the wheel. This must be normal!

As we continued dodging speeding vehicles, David explained this was an area called Venda Nova, a typical neighborhood for the working class. When we slowed down, I saw a lot of raw red earth and unfinished houses with cement gray roofs. The road was full of pot-holes, and the buses belched great clouds of black diesel smoke.

We stayed at Betânia for a few days. We were introduced to all the missionaries, and among them were George and Dolly Foster. He was a big, tall guy with a barrel chest, a bald head, thick glasses, and a calm, confident air. Dolly was trim, pretty, and bubbly. On our second day, George asked if I wanted to speak at Peniel, a church in the city. He would translate for me. I readily agreed, and when Sunday came, George and Pam and I got into the car and headed downtown. It was our first real look at Belo Horizonte. I was surprised how modern the buildings were and how wide the avenues. Quite different from Venda Nova. A beautiful park was situated in the middle of town, filled with ponds and poinciana trees with orange blossoms.

The church service was wonderful, with what must have been four hundred to five hundred enthusiastic young people in attendance. They worshiped the Lord with guitars and Brazilian rhythm. I preached with George as my interpreter, and it seemed like the reaction was favorable. Hundreds of faces looked up at me, waiting for each sentence to be interpreted. I loved it here and felt good about being in Brazil.

Later we stepped out of the church into the cool night. George went to get the car and drove us over to a fast-food place where we could get a snack.

"*Moleque!*"

I turned to my right and saw a small mob on the streets, yelling and shaking their arms. Pam and I took a few steps in the direction of the commotion. "What is it, George?" Then I saw a skinny brown boy in the middle of the melee. He might have been ten years old. We approached the crowd, careful to stay in the background.

"They're accusing him of stealing something," explained George. "He's denying it. This kind of thing happens a lot here. He's a street kid—what we call *meninos de rua.*"

We hurried on to George's car. As we sped down the darkened streets, he said something that shocked and saddened us. "These *meninos de rua* live their whole lives on the street, begging, stealing…some sell themselves as male prostitutes," said George. My thoughts went back to the little boy standing defiant against so many grown-ups.

George went on, "They're a real problem. They're not orphans; most come from single-parent, poor families...if you could call them families. They go out on the streets to make their own way as early as five or six years of age. Some estimate there are three million of them in Brazil, living on the streets. They're almost all on drugs of some kind...sniffing glue is the most popular. Half of them are dead before they grow up."

I looked out the car window as we drove through the city. I peered closely down side alleys and in dark corners of the town squares, called praças, and caught a glimpse of some boys and girls. A few huddled around a fire, and others curled up to sleep on the broken pavement underneath cardboard or rags. I could hardly stand it. Three million like this? Could anyone help them?

Within a few days, I was worried about our own survival. It started when we tagged along with David to meet our language teacher. Lillian was a warm, smiling young woman who spoke conversational English with an attractive Latin accent. We sat in her parlor and worked out the details of our Portuguese studies. We'd study with her four hours a day, five days a week. Then we could spend the rest of our time by ourselves doing homework. That would help us learn Portuguese as soon as possible so we could get on with our work. Everything seemed to be falling into place.

Then David turned to Lillian. "I've told Jim and Pam their lessons would cost $50 a month."

Lillian's face flushed a little, and she seemed unable to make eye contact, looking instead at the floor. A prolonged silence ensued. "Actually, David, I must not have been as clear as I should have been. I charge by the hour. If one person were to study one hour a day, then the total would come to $50 a month. But there are two of them, and they want to study four hours a day. That would bring the total to $400 a month."

Oh no! With all my worrying, I'd never considered this possibility. Our language study alone was going to cost eight times our regular monthly support. What were we going to do? David looked confused and embarrassed. I still wasn't able to say anything. David stammered for words. "I don't think they can pay that much," he finally said.

I nodded. "That's right. We don't have that kind of support." My understatement was very close to a lie. "We'll have to think about cutting down on classes a bit."

The painful conversation stretched on. We finally agreed to study two hours a day at the regular rate, and Lillian offered a bonus hour free with her sister, Vivian. That still left us with a projected study expense four times greater than our projected income!

SEVEN

"Trust Me and Keep Going"

DAVID was still apologizing as we got into his car to go see our new home. We couldn't afford to rent a house of our own, so the plan was for us to stay with a Brazilian family and pay room and board. I hoped this arrangement would work better than our language lesson agreement.

We drove three blocks and pulled up in front of a house that was perched on a steep hillside and was blackened with mildew. Not much was left of its grayish-white paint, but it looked better than what I had feared. The neighborhood looked pleasant.

We followed David around the corner of the house and down some crumbling concrete steps that were also dark with mildew. Although the house only had one story on the street side, back here were two stories. David said Pam and I would have a room underneath, on the hillside.

David knocked on the door, and we were greeted by a beaming woman, not five feet tall in high heels. She didn't speak English, yet she projected such warmth and love that I felt immediately at ease. Here was a woman who exuded Jesus even as she ushered us inside. We entered the living room with its beautiful hardwood floors and formal furniture. Dona Lica, our hostess, directed us to straight-backed chairs. David would translate for us. We had little to discuss, and so we immediately talked dollars and cents.

When David explained that I was willing to pay the agreed-to $70 a month for room and board, Dona Lica reacted much the same as Lillian had. Her smile evaporated, and she looked troubled. *Oh no*, I thought. *Don't tell me it's happening again!*

She fidgeted in her chair as she talked to David. His face reddened as he translated her words. "It seems there has been a misunderstanding. The $70 was for one person. Since there are two, the cost is double: $140." I sat there, dumbfounded. I couldn't look at Pam. What were we going to do?

"Jim, I'm so sorry for the mistakes. I really don't know what to say. I...I hope this doesn't cause you too many problems," said David.

"It's all right, David. We appreciate your help." Inside my thoughts were screaming, *Too many problems? These aren't problems, these are disasters! What are we going to do ?*

David and Dona Lica talked for a little while in Portuguese, then he turned to us again. "She can't make any decisions without talking to her husband, but she'll see if they might be able to give you a discount."

David left, and we walked down the hallway to our room. It was very small and painted a depressing shade of deep blue. Patches of bright pink were evident where the blue paint had peeled. The best feature was a window that opened on a hillside view of Belo Horizonte and a lot of sky. The only furniture was a bed frame with a piece of foam rubber for a mattress and a wardrobe for our clothes.

Pam sank onto the bed and burst into tears. I gave her a few ineffective pats on the shoulder. I could think of nothing to say; besides, the big knot in my throat blocked any words I might have considered. If I tried to speak, I would cry, too. I retreated to the bathroom down the hall. Even that offered no consolation. After using the toilet I reached out to flush it, and water gushed from the wall under the wash basin, spraying over my shoes and splashing my pants. I peered under the basin. A pipe had fallen off the wall and was shooting water all over me and the room. I stuck my finger in the pipe. The flow temporarily stopped, but now what? I kept my finger in the pipe and stretched as far as I could, trying to reach the door to unlock it and call for help. But I couldn't reach that far! I stood helpless, not even knowing the Portuguese words to yell for assistance.

Finally, I managed to replace the pipe, pushing it back far enough so that it didn't fall out. By then I was soaking wet and not feeling good about my missionary calling. I could think of just one thing to do: Pray. I went outside and sat down on the crumbly black steps.

"Lord, this is awful," I complained. "How could I have brought Pam down here? What are we going to do? We can't afford to stay, but we don't have a ticket home. I don't see any way we're going to be able to pay our bills. That alone is a terrible testimony, and it will bring shame to YWAM and to You, Lord."

The past few years had taught me to recognize inner dialogue with God. His voice came quietly into my mind.

Who called you here?

"I thought it was You, Lord. Now I'm pretty confused."

Did I confirm to your leaders that you should be allowed to come to Brazil and pioneer YWAM?

"Yes, they seemed to think so."

Did I do several last-minute miracles to get you here?

"Yes, it sure seemed so, Lord."

If I got you here, don't you think I can take care of you?

"I've always believed that, Lord; at least in theory. Now it's all so real. Here we are thousands of miles from home. Everything is so strange. I can't make a phone call. I can't understand the language. Our financial situation is ridiculous. I feel as if I've lost all control of my own life!"

Good. You have lost control because I am in control. You're here because I brought you here. Trust Me and keep going, Jim.

"Father, I don't know how good I am at trusting, but I can keep going. That doesn't take much talent. I can do that. Lord, I won't quit. I don't like much about Brazil right now, but You brought us here, and we're going to obey You."

I got up and went inside, bracing myself to face my wife, whom I had left crying on the bed. When I got to the room she was all unpacked and bustling around, singing songs with a big smile on her face!

"Jim, I noticed when we were at Betânia that they are doing a lot of painting," she said. "Do you think someone might let us have some leftover paint to redo this room?"

Within a few days our situation had brightened considerably. Our room was a light, cheery yellow, we were attending Portuguese class, and we were starting to get to know our hosts. Lillian encouraged us, and the family we were staying with was delightful, although we couldn't understand one another yet. God had surrounded us with wonderful, supportive people.

The language study was difficult, though, and we occasionally struggled with bouts of isolation. The financial situation preyed on my mind, and I had to have at least two-and-a-half hours of prayer every day to bring myself up to a level of mild depression.

I tried to suppress questions such as: Are we actually accomplishing anything? What would be our next step after we learned the basics of Portuguese? How would we catch the attention of Brazilian young people?

I had to trust that God had the answers to all my questions and would reveal them in His time. One of the answers took the form of a post office box.

Before we arrived in Brazil, Rudy Lack had collected some stories about YWAM's work in other parts of the world and had given them to Betânia to distribute. Betânia was preparing to publish these stories in its magazine, *Mensagem da Cruz*, and someone suggested that my name and address accompany the articles. This way, Brazilian youth who were interested in learning more about YWAM would know how to reach us. A friend loaned us the use of his post office box, since we didn't have a permanent address.

More good news: We heard that Loren Cunningham, YWAM's founder and director, was coming to Brazil to speak to a conference of missionaries in São Paulo. That would give us the opportunity to become acquainted with area missionaries and to talk with Loren about how best we could introduce Brazilians to YWAM. The only problem was that we didn't have the money to travel to São Paulo or to pay the conference fees. All we could do was pray.

Our prayers were answered a few days before the conference when we were invited to dinner with a missionary from New Zealand. He picked us up and drove us across town to the mission center where he and his wife lived. I looked at the two-story L-shaped building and wondered if we would ever have enough YWAMers to occupy a place like this.

During our evening together our host told us he had recently sold a car, and he and his wife wanted to give us part of the tithe. We decided to use it to attend the conference in São Paulo.

EIGHT

A Lonely Vision

T H E hotel that served as conference headquarters wasn't deluxe, but we were delighted by its beautiful location, the pleasant staff who spoke English, and the "creature comforts" we hadn't enjoyed in several weeks. We registered, found our room, and headed for the pool. We didn't know it, but we would need the hours of relaxation to prepare us for the bad news we would encounter the next morning when we went in search of Loren.

"Sorry. I thought you'd heard," said the man in charge of the conference the next day. "Loren isn't coming to speak after all. It seems he's had trouble with his voice. In fact, he could barely talk on the phone." With that he walked away and left us standing there.

If Loren wasn't coming, what were we doing here? Should we save the little money we had by hurrying home? We decided to wait and see if God had another reason for us to be in São Paulo. Later that afternoon an older missionary, dressed in tropical whites, came up to us and began a conversation. He assumed we were the children of missionary delegates to the conference. "It's great to see young people at a meeting like this," he said. "Who are your parents?"

"Well, we do have parents," I replied, "but they're back in the United States. We're here as missionaries with YWAM—Youth With a Mission."

"Never heard of them," he said in his booming voice. "What is it you think you'll be doing here?"

"We've just arrived in Brazil. Our goal is to mobilize and train young people for world evangelism."

"*Brazilian* young people?"

"Yes." I was at a loss. Why couldn't *Brazilian* young people be trained for missionary work? Disapproval was evident on his face as he asked his next question.

"Are you going to use both men *and* women?"

"Yes. That's our plan."

"How much will you pay them?"

"No, you don't understand. We don't want employees. We want colleagues. They are to be our equals in the mission and will have to depend on God for their support, just as we do."

He shook his head in disbelief. I knew he wasn't challenging us or trying to be difficult. He was an experienced missionary and had probably been here his entire professional life. The fact that he found our goal incredible worried me. Still, I plunged ahead.

"We believe God has guided us here. He will provide for our needs and for those who are called to work with us." I realized that my words sounded hopelessly unrealistic and super-spiritual. But the answer was the best I could muster.

"Son, you're headed for disaster. Brazilians won't work for you if you don't pay them. And if you have guys and girls together, there will be a lot of immorality. Their churches aren't going to support them, either. Money will be a real problem because Brazilians don't have much vision for missions."

Was this the message we had traveled so far to hear? Was he right? It was discouraging to have our vision pronounced impossible by a veteran in the field. What's more, over the next several days we heard the same misgivings repeated by a number of seasoned missionaries. Then the conference was over.

I didn't have time to be discouraged for long. A challenging invitation awaited me when we returned to Betânia. Loren Cunningham had been scheduled to speak at a citywide missions rally in Belo Horizonte following the conference for the missionaries. Betânia had gone all out preparing for the rally. When Loren had to cancel because of losing his voice, I figured the Belo rally would also be called off.

Two days before the rally, George asked me if I would speak in Loren's place. My palms got sweaty. Could I speak at a citywide rally? To hundreds of people? Could I fill in for an international missions leader like Loren Cunningham? In spite of my misgivings, I accepted and agreed to try my best.

During the next two days I spent a lot of time praying and leafing through my Bible. I heard that my translator at the rally would be the same man who had translated for Billy Graham in Rio de Janeiro. This did little to calm my nerves. Loren Cunningham! Billy Graham! Jim Stier? I was definitely out of my league. Apparently I wasn't the only one to think so.

"If I had known Loren wasn't coming, I might have stayed home, too," the interpreter said as I joined him in the car bound for the rally. He had as much faith in me as I had in myself.

I put myself in the Lord's hands and preached. The interpreter did a great job. Of the six hundred young people in attendance, about two hundred accepted my challenge to come to the front as a sign they were willing to go out in missions.

I looked around at them, their heads bowed earnestly in prayer. *I didn't preach that well*, I thought. *This must have been God...it sure wasn't me.* The interpreter turned to me and smiled.

"We had a very good meeting," he said simply.

A few days later I was invited to speak for a week at Betânia's Bible school. When the school director, Larry Darby, came to pick us up, I knew I had met a friend. Pam, Larry, and I talked nonstop for the three hours it took to get to our destination. His high energy level and his enthusiasm about the Lord were just what we needed to buoy our spirits and replenish our determination.

We had a good week teaching and getting to know Larry better. But even he told us we would never be able to do what we were proposing. We felt very alone in our vision. Could we be right and all these missionaries—even someone like Larry—be wrong? I didn't know of anyone who had done what we wanted to do. Maybe it *was* impossible.

NINE

Always Enough

MONEY was our most pressing concern, and each day's trip to Post Office Box 2024 held the promise of a miracle. Our church in Hawaii had raised our support level several times during our early months in Brazil. What had started as $50 a month grew to $150 and then to $250. As wonderful and faithful as the offerings were, they didn't meet our needs.

We were aware that if we couldn't pay our bills, other people would suffer. Our language teacher was wonderfully flexible, generous, and helpful, and only made us pay for the times we were there. However, she and her family depended on her income, and any absences on our part put a strain on their budget. Similarly, the family where we boarded lowered our rent from $140 to $100, although they were constructing an apartment building for their children and were stretched to the limit financially.

In spite of everyone's kindness and generosity—several Brazilians gave us offerings, which was very unusual—we needed miracles. Our bills were $300 a month, and our support hadn't reached that level yet. And so, I often prayed over the situation as I made my daily trek into Belo Horizonte to pick up the mail.

I remember one Friday in particular when our room and board fees were due and we were down to a few coins. It was a beautiful sunny day, but how could I enjoy it? Here we were, faced with financial failure…again. My stomach was in knots as I walked down the last steep hill toward the downtown area where the post office was located. Poverty was everywhere—street kids, beggars, rag pickers—as I pushed my way through the crowd, entered the post office, and headed to Box 2024.

"What in the world?" I muttered when I saw the overflow of envelopes. Most of them were from Brazil, probably responses to the article in Betânia's magazine. Then I noticed an American stamp and tore open the envelope. A check fluttered to the floor. I looked in disbelief at the amount: $100. That was exactly what we needed to pay for our room and board! Kenny, a young man who had participated in a Bible study course I had taught in Hawaii, explained the gift in his note:

> Dear Jim,
>
> I was at the airport working. It was my day to take care of a conveyer belt that transports garbage. As I was standing there watching it, a $100 bill passed by right in front of me. I snatched it up and took it to lost and found, as we are supposed to do. A couple of weeks later I was called in. No one had claimed the money, which meant it was mine. I prayed and asked the Lord what I should do with it. He seemed to tell me I should send it to you right away.
>
> Do you think I heard from God?
>
> Kenny

A tremendous warmth swelled within me as I stood there. Everything in this new country was strange and vaguely threatening, but God was there, and He was taking care of us. I felt ashamed of my worries. I walked back to our house, praying quietly all the way. "Please forgive my disbelief, Father. You are more than powerful enough to provide for us. You are more than loving enough to do it, and You are more than faithful enough to never fail. Help me to believe more, Lord."

I could hardly wait to tell Pam, but when I explained our miracle, she gave me that same serene look that I had come to admire so much. "Of course God provided for us, Jim," she said. "We knew He would." She was right, as usual. My disbelief dishonored Him, and I felt ashamed.

❧ ❧ ❧ ❧

Just as the Lord worked through friends such as Kenny to provide us with miracles, so He worked through us to help others. Shortly after our experience at the post office, we had an opportunity to assist the Lord with His work.

A group of four YWAMers, two of them Brazilians, visited us from Argentina. They had attended a training school taught by Wedge and Shirley and were on their way to a mission assignment near the Amazon. During their stay we learned they were totally broke. As I prayed for them, I felt God nudging me to give them an offering. We actually had the money early that month for our room and board. If I was hearing right, the Lord wanted us to give all we had—$100.

Pam thought it was a good idea to give them our rent money. But I struggled. Wasn't it irresponsible to give away what little we had when our bills were due in two weeks, and others depended on us to meet our commitments? I was caught in indecision. As the time approached for the missionary team to leave, I sat by the window and prayed in earnest. God's message came to me very clearly.

At that moment Dona Lica came down the hall calling me. The team was there to say goodbye. Pam said, "Wait a minute, guys. We want to send something with you." She had baked some cookies and had packed them in a shoebox. I slipped in the money and handed the package to the closest team member, a young Brazilian named Gerson. He thanked me and told me he was planning to stay with YWAM in Argentina after the jungle trip. We shook hands all around, and the team headed out the door unaware of the "miracle" the box contained. But we knew about it, and we felt good that we had obeyed God.

A few days later we received an offering from the youth group at a local church. The amount totaled exactly the sum we had put in with the cookies: $100.

Not all miracles involve money. One afternoon Pam and I were downtown walking along the crowded streets. It was Saturday and we were on a break from our language studies. Although I didn't say anything out loud, I found myself wishing I could treat Pam to a movie or lunch at a restaurant. We hadn't had a "date" since our arrival. However, I was learning to scale down dreams, and I had a "Plan B" in mind.

"Guess what," I said, squeezing her hand. "I've hoarded our riches, and we can go wild and buy two Cokes!" She looked skeptical.

"Sure you can handle that, big spender?" she joked.

"Only if you promise not to get used to such excesses," I replied. I jingled a couple of coins in my pocket. "A person has to have a fling once in a while." At that moment, a young man tapped me on the shoulder.

"Excuse me," he said. "I couldn't help overhearing your English. My name is Teófilo. I am learning English and I like to practice. Could I take you out for lunch or something?"

Pam and I exchanged glances, wondering if we should be grateful or suspicious. We nodded and Teófilo hailed a cab that took us to the nicest part of the city. We hadn't ridden in a taxi since our arrival, and we had never been to the good side of town. Here the apartment buildings were new, and sidewalk cafés lined the streets. Young, fashionable couples ate and drank and laughed in the sunshine.

Our host selected an Arabian restaurant where we feasted on lamb, rice pilaf, and homemade flat bread. Later we went to watch an American film. It was such a luxury to listen to English and see familiar scenes from the States. For a couple of hours we forgot the pressures and strangeness of our circumstances. Afterward, Teófilo took us home, and we never saw him again. But during the evening he told us his name meant "friend of God." We don't know where he came from or where he went, but he was God's provision for us that Saturday. The Lord had provided us with diversion.

Diversion wouldn't save souls, though. I wrestled with how to start YWAM in Brazil. I'd had experiences in other places but wondered if the same strategies would work here. I guessed we should start with some kind of training. But where? When? Would Brazilians join us, or would they be unwilling to work without pay, as the missionaries had predicted.

I reminded myself that a lot of young people had responded when I had filled in for Loren Cunningham at the missions rally. And I had encountered real enthusiasm at the churches I had visited in the area. So far, though, not a single Brazilian had talked to us about joining our ministry. I couldn't blame them because we didn't exactly know what we would be doing.

Then we met Marcelo.

He didn't look like a prospective missionary. With his shoulder-length hair, bushy beard, and piercing eyes he resembled a castoff from a hippie love-in. We invited him over to our room to continue a conversation begun at church. We offered him the only chair we had, and we plunked down on the edge of the bed to hear his story.

He told us he used to live in New York City. It had been a wild life, full of drugs, sex, and violence. One day he resisted a man who held him up in Central Park and was knifed in the stomach. Medics rushed him to a hospital where he was taken immediately into surgery. "But it was too late," he explained, watching us as if gauging our reaction to his next words. "I died on the operating table. Then I saw Jesus. He showed me heaven and hell. I thought I was finished. Then Jesus said

I could return. Suddenly I was back in my body, on the operating table. They had resuscitated me."

I looked at Pam, who was caught up in the drama of the story. As far-out as his words sounded, I believed that this young man was telling the truth. He went on to explain that the Lord had told him to return to Brazil. "I'm working with a church, helping drug addicts, but somehow I think there's something else I'm meant to do."

Could this be our first Brazilian co-worker? I certainly hoped so.

Marcelo started coming over regularly, and we went out a few times to talk to people about Jesus. Our limited command of Portuguese frustrated us as we tried to share the gospel. After one such foray into the field, we came back to our room to hear the news we had been waiting to hear.

"I've been praying a lot," began Marcelo. "I think the Lord wants me to be with YWAM."

We saw this as an important sign that the Lord was ready for us to launch our ministry. This fact was confirmed by the envelopes that stuffed our mailbox in response to the articles in Betânia's magazine. We tallied more than five hundred letters, all written in Portuguese, of course. We redoubled our efforts to learn the language. Our teacher, Lillian, and her sister, Vivian, helped us in more ways than one. Vivian translated the letters for us and offered to help us write a form letter in response. But what should we say?

Pam and I spent several days praying intensely. Finally we formed our plan. We would start our first program five months from now on December 29, 1975. That would be during summer vacation here, south of the equator. We'd start with one month of training, giving the most basic stuff we had learned in our school in Hawaii. Then we'd break them into teams and send them out to evangelize in Brazil. The only question was, where should we do the training? Again, Lillian came through. She suggested we arrange to use a Bible college during its summer break. That put some urgency into our language studies.

Administrators at the local Bible college agreed to rent us their facility. We sent the letters announcing the summer program and soon had thirty-five confirmed participants. We hoped some of these would want to stay on after the summer and form a permanent staff.

In mid-December Pam and I left the home where we had been boarding and moved into the Bible school. Moving was more of an emotional than a logistical problem. We had only two suitcases, two sleeping bags, and a guitar, but the family with whom we had lived for eight months had become very special, and our little yellow room was comfortable and secure. We would only be able to stay in the Bible school until the end of January. Where would we live after that? We would have to trust God for the answer.

We worked hard getting the school ready for our young missionary candidates. It had been empty for more than a month and needed a lot of repairs.

We chose for ourselves a room with a private bath. However, since the roofing over our room was only thin sheets of pressed cement and fiber, when the summer sun beat down, it easily reached 110 degrees inside.

December was hot and rainy in Brazil. Christmas and heat still seemed incompatible to me, but at least Pam's folks would be coming from Hawaii for the holidays. Pam was so excited, and I tried not to worry about showing her folks exactly how their daughter was living.

We arranged for them to stay at Betânia, but they saw the hot room that was our home, and a temporary one at that. I knew her dad must have worried that we didn't have a vehicle. Every time we wanted to do anything together, I had to borrow a car from Betânia. They said very little, though. Then just before they left, and a few days before we started our program, my father-in-law broached the subject.

"Jim, couldn't you leave YWAM and transfer to Betânia?"

I answered him in a noncommittal way, but I had to admit the idea had appeal. Betânia was established. The people there lived well and were making an impact with their publications and Bible schools. They were dedicated people, too, and everything they did was high quality. As for us, the only visible evidence of our efforts was a pile of letters and Marcelo's commitment to join us.

TEN

A Force for His Kingdom

I HAD ignored a worsening chest cold while Pam's folks were with us, and the morning we took them to the airport, I woke up feeling awful. As soon as we waved goodbye, I hurried back to our room at the Bible college.

It was a hot day, and I was drenched with sweat. Every breath stabbed my chest as I flopped on the bed. This was terrible! Our program started in three days. We didn't have a thermometer, but I knew I had a high fever. After a few hours I felt as if I were breathing through glue.

Pam suspected pneumonia and insisted that we call a doctor. I refused. We had no money for a doctor, I said as I lay there wheezing in the oppressive heat and staring at the pink walls. I wondered how I would ever have the strength to lead the school in a few days.

That afternoon I heard Pam tiptoe in and come over to the bed. Then she was rubbing something damp on my upper arm. I was

77

annoyed. I was about to open my eyes and complain when suddenly I felt the jab of a needle in my arm.

"Ow! What are you doing?" I tried to yank my arm away.

"Hold still, would you? I got some penicillin at the drugstore. They sell it here without a prescription. Don't worry, it was cheap."

"Well, you could have at least warned me. Look at my arm! It looks like there's a tennis ball under the skin."

"Oh, Jim. It's not that bad. Anyway, if you hadn't jumped, it wouldn't be like that. If you're too stubborn to go to the doctor, then you have to take what you can get."

I started to get better but was still in bed when our students began to arrive. It was my duty as the director of the school to greet them. As they trickled in, Pam brought them one by one into our room. There I lay. I knew what they were thinking. The powerful man of God they expected from reading those articles in Betânia's magazine was nowhere to be found. Instead, there was this wheezing, sweaty, pallid lump on the bed. Every recruit had the same uncertain smile, as if to say, "What am I getting into?"

I asked them if they planned to stay after the initial two-month program. I can't remember one answering in the affirmative. Judging from the looks on their faces, most wondered if I would last that long.

My impressions of them were mixed, too.

There was Graça Carvalho. Larry Darby, our friend from the Bible school, dropped her off, but first he came in alone and apologized for leaving her with us. She hadn't done well academically at Betânia and had a bad attitude. "I don't know where else to put her," he confessed. "I hope you have better luck with her than we did." Graça looked nice enough to me. She was shy and seemed unremarkable.

A while later Pam ushered in a short, skinny guy. I wondered for a moment if he were old enough to attend the school. He didn't say much and seemed a little scared. His eyes were big behind his glasses, and his Adam's apple kept bobbing up and down. He introduced himself as Jaime Araújo and told me he'd left a good job to come. Probably the reality of what he'd done was finally sinking in.

"Are you planning to stay on after the training program, Jaime?"

He didn't answer. He just stared at me and mumbled something I couldn't quite understand with my limited Portuguese.

Another young man had come from the city of Campos. He seemed like a good prospect, but when I asked if he was interested in a missions career, he explained he had just finished his college entrance exams. If he didn't pass, he might continue with us.

One of the girls said she had been facing a real crossroads in her life. Should she check herself into a psychiatric hospital or come to YWAM? We won out and here she was, trying to patch her life together.

A journalist came. He was fleeing the Communists in his home country of Mozambique. When we put him to work with some of the cleaning we hadn't finished—scrubbing bathrooms—Pam found him crying like a baby. He had never done menial labor in his life.

Marcelo was another arrival. I was beginning to rely on this intense young man with the long hair and beard.

We had expected thirty-five, but only twenty-two showed up, and they were a real ragtag army. It looked as if we might well fulfill the fate almost every missionary or responsible adult had predicted for us. Only God could help us now and form us into a force for His kingdom.

Rudy Lack and Wedge and Shirley Alman came to teach in the first school. It was encouraging to see someone else from YWAM. They helped make the school a success, challenging the young people to radical commitment to Jesus. Our school also had times of intense group prayer with a lot of tears, confession of sin, and repentance. Every day we broke the students into small groups to pray for the nations of the world. During these times they were supposed to listen to God until He gave them direction for their prayers.

Sometimes they came back with wild reports. For example, one group prayed for a car for YWAM. They said God showed them it would be a blue Volkswagen van, and so they prayed for the money to buy it. Then one girl had a vision of a van catching fire in the middle of the street. They prayed until they were sure they had overcome that danger.

I smiled and didn't say anything. They were a bit naive—first-timers at trying to hear the voice of God. I didn't want to discourage them from stepping out in faith. Marcelo was a great help, demonstrating strong leadership qualities. We put him in charge of one of the teams.

At the end of January our students went off in three teams to minister during February. Meanwhile, Pam and I had some decisions to make. One day Pam asked the question that had been echoing in my head.

"Jim, I can't visualize what our ministry will be like after the teams come back. What will we be doing?"

I didn't know how to answer her.

We didn't have a place to conduct training except during summer holidays. And because the economy was so poor, we probably couldn't travel around with teams as we had in the United States. We didn't have a place to live ourselves, much less house other workers. We would have to continue in a walk of faith, always a step away from disaster.

We still had a few weeks before we had to move, so I traveled to visit the teams. Marcelo's group was in a town called Diamantina, about five hours away. When I got off the bus, all seven were there to greet me.

"It's been incredible, Jim! Several young people have come to the Lord. The pastor is very happy!" Marcelo was glowing. The others chimed in with stories of all that had happened. They found out it was a tough town with a lot of supernatural oppression. At first, it had been hard to talk to people about the Lord and difficult to pray.

"One house had really strange things happening to it," Marcelo said. "The people heard heavy things falling on their roof. They ran out to see what it was." Marcelo paused, looking at me. "Rocks were raining on their house, out of the sky. The rocks were burning hot." I took this in, remembering what others had told me about bizarre occult experiences in this country.

"The bishop came to do an exorcism, but the strange stuff kept happening. Then we met these people while going from house to house and prayed with them to accept Christ. Our whole team went over later and prayed. All the strange things stopped happening to that house," Marcelo finished.

"Did you actually see any of that happen?" I asked, trying not to look too unbelieving. "Or did you just hear them talk about it?"

"No, we were there when it happened, and we held the hot rocks in our hands!"

No wonder they were excited.

I watched during the few days I was there. The place where the team was staying was constantly filled with people coming to ask how to know Jesus. I was proud of them. The other teams I visited were much the same.

Back in Belo Horizonte, Pam and I looked at several houses. Those that were large enough were too expensive. Those with low rent were too small. What would we do? Then Pam contracted a virus something like mononucleosis.

This time I scraped up the money for a doctor, and he said she needed complete bed rest. All I could think of was that soon she would have no bed!

The teams came back. Pam got up to sit with me and listen to their reports. At least fifty people had come to the Lord, demons had been cast out, and churches had grown. I looked around at the members of our group. They were all amazed at how God had used them. It reminded me of the scene in the Bible when the seventy came back, excitedly telling Jesus all that had happened. We sent them to their homes to pray about returning as full-time staff. How many would accept our invitation? And where would they come back to?

Then George Foster found a possible place not far from Betânia. As we pulled up in front, I was impressed. The street was paved and a bus stop was nearby. The house was Portuguese colonial—white with arched windows, red roof tiles, and doors trimmed in blue. There was a patch of lawn out front. Inside were four bedrooms. A small master bedroom with a bath and an outside entrance would give Pam and me privacy. Also, two servants' quarters were out in the big backyard.

It looked so good. I cringed when I heard the price— $450 a month, more than the sum of all our regular support. The owner, a Christian, listened sympathetically as I explained our situation. He offered to give us some months at reduced rent. He promised to prepare a contract. I returned a few days later by bus. The house looked even better in the bright sunshine. I stood out front and, in Brazilian fashion, clapped my hands so the owner would know I had arrived.

He greeted me warmly and ushered me into the dining room, where the contract was waiting on a table. I sat down and began to read the Portuguese carefully. As I made my way through the text, my hands turned clammy and my stomach tightened. It was all there in black and white. The owner was giving us two months at a slightly reduced rate. Our church had recently raised our support to $400 a month, but I was still committing us to paying a rent higher than our whole income. How would we eat? However, it was either rent this house or stop every-thing and lose the momentum we had gained in our first program.

The real question was whether or not we wanted to take on the load of new workers. We could easily send them away. Pam and I could live within our means, preach in churches, and take out volunteers in the summer. I sat there staring at the contract. God had called us to enable Brazilians to be missionaries. If we weren't willing to take risks, we couldn't challenge them to do the same. Still, I'd better warn the owner before I signed.

"Sir, we need a place like this, and I'm ready to sign the contract. You should know, though, that we live by faith. We don't have enough promised income to pay this. I believe God will supply, but you should know our circumstances."

"No problem," he said, beaming. "As a matter of fact, I like the idea of renting to an American."

I knew he didn't believe me when I told him we had very little income. He thought we must be rich Americans. I took up the pen, breathed a silent prayer, and signed.

We got Pam settled right away, and though she was feeling better now, it was good to have a place where she could rest. We found some used furniture, a stove, and a refrigerator. Pam's parents also decided to help us, shipping some wedding presents that we hadn't given away, as well as our bedroom furniture, a television, and even an air conditioner. I had to go to Rio several times to guide the shipments through customs, but what a difference it made to have some comforts from home. Our Betânia friends gave us a housewarming, including a rectangular rug that was turquoise with black trim. We proudly laid it in the living room.

A few days later the students started trickling back. Twelve returned to work with us. We were ready to start. The only question was, what would we do with them? I looked around at our group gathered in the living room of the new house: Marcelo, with his full beard and long hair; Graça, with all her problems; the girl who had chosen us over a mental hospital; Jaime, too, who had turned out to be a solid guy, even though he looked to be only about fifteen years old.

Clearly we were not going to be overwhelmed with invitations from churches. I didn't think I would have invited us myself if I had been a pastor! I thought about publishing some pamphlets to start promoting the mission but decided God wanted us to spread the gospel first. The only plan I could devise was to pray a lot and witness on the streets every day.

We agreed to a schedule: We would get up at 5:30 for devotions. Everyone meditated on the same Scriptures, getting together afterward to share the results. Then we would pray for the nations. After chores and lunch, we would catch the bus for the forty-minute ride downtown, followed by a fifteen-minute walk to the park. There we would break into pairs and share our faith with unbelievers until evening.

The park with its orange flowering trees, trails, and ponds was a haven for all sorts. People escaped the heat of the day on benches in the shade. All we had to do was walk up and start a conversation. Most were happy to talk. The park was also a hangout for drug users, homosexuals, street kids, and thieves. We talked with them, too.

Getting home was a challenge. The line for the bus was more than a block long, and it often took a couple of hours to get back in the evening. Despite the long hours, we began to feel Brazil was home. Pam loved animals, and soon we had a cat and a pet turtle. We also began to take in some of the street people to try to give them a chance to change their lives.

That's how Claudete found a home with us. It was almost a fatal mistake. Claudete had been arrested on many occasions, sometimes because of drugs and sometimes as a suspect in subversion cases against the military dictatorship. One Sunday afternoon I was trying to deal with some problems in her life. Pam was in the house, but Claudete and I sat alone in our sparsely furnished living room, talking. As I probed for reasons for her erratic behavior, Claudete shifted from one side of the sofa to the other. Then she shocked me.

"I have a good friend who lives inside me," she said.

"What do you mean? Is this an imaginary friend, another expression of you, or what?"

She shook her head vehemently. "None of that. He's a real person, and he lives in my body with me."

Scooting to the edge of my seat, I looked closely at Claudete. "How did he get there?"

"It was one of the times I was in jail. This time I was in big trouble. The police left me alone in a cold, dark cell for three days. They didn't even give me food. I knew I was facing a long prison term. I was desperate. Then *he* came to me in that dark cell. He looked like an angel of light. He said if I would let him live in my body, he would bring me food. He would also get me out of prison. I agreed and he left. A while later he was back with food. Then he came into me. He has been with me ever since."

Her voice was so flat in that bare living room. I felt cold.

"A few days later I was sentenced to a long term and sent to the penitentiary. But when I arrived, some of my papers from the jail were missing. The warden was so angry. He said he was going to show them they couldn't be sloppy like that, and he let me go."

I looked at her earnestly. "Claudete, that sounds like a demonic spirit to me. If you want to follow Jesus, the spirit has to go."

She twisted on the sofa, her eyes fixed on the turquoise and black rug. "He doesn't want to leave. He'd have to go to a place where it's gray and cold."

"Can I cast him out? It's necessary if you want to follow Jesus."

"I guess so."

By now she looked scared, and she squirmed as if she were sitting on a hot stove. I suggested we walk in the backyard awhile. I put my hand on her head there in the garden and commanded the spirit to leave. I only prayed a short time, but felt that it had gone. I opened my eyes and looked at Claudete. Amazement, anger, fear, and sadness flitted across her face in rapid succession.

"He says he is going to destroy you," she said. "He is the Bandit of the Amazon. He is from the Seven Currents of Allah and is a very powerful spirit."

"He can't destroy me. Let me explain something." I took a stick and scratched a line in the dirt. "I'm in the kingdom of God, over here. He's in the kingdom of darkness, over there. He can't invade my side, but I can invade his. I'm under the protection of Jesus, and he can't touch me. You don't have that protection unless you repent and turn to Jesus, asking Him into your heart. Can you do that today, Claudete?"

She prayed, but when we were done she said, "I wish you hadn't cast him out. I miss him. He was my best friend."

Claudete withdrew more and more. We knew the evil spirit was back, but she never let us get close enough to help again. Then tragedy threatened.

Because we suffered chronic water shortages, we put extra tanks in the attic to store water when the city managed to pump a little up to our street. We weren't experts, though. One of the tanks we installed sprung a bad leak, and water was pouring out of it. We had a mess. One of the girls' rooms was right below the tank. When the water came pouring through the ceiling, the girls abandoned their beds in the middle of the night and went to the living room to sleep.

The next morning, Pam woke me.

"Last night I woke up in the middle of the night. I felt like I should pray for the safety of our girls."

"Really?" I mumbled, trying to get fully awake.

"After about a half hour, I felt I could go back to sleep."

I didn't think any more about what Pam had said until we got to breakfast. One of the girls took us aside. "Jim, last night while we were sleeping in the living room, I saw something strange. It was Claudete." She paused and looked across the room to where Claudete was sipping her coffee. "She was roaming from room to room. I kept real quiet and watched. She had a big knife. I saw it in the light from the street."

When Pam and I confronted Claudete, she immediately confessed to doing it.

"I got up to kill Rosane, but she wasn't in her room. I couldn't find her."

She seemed sort of sorry, but it was obvious we couldn't risk allowing her to stay with the group. One day we left her at home while we went downtown to evangelize. When we came home, Claudete was gone. She had strangled Pam's cat, killed the turtle, and stolen several items from the girls. We never saw her again.

ELEVEN

Defeat into Victory

P A M   continued to have health problems. She had bouts with elusive viruses that left her weakened and tired. She never complained, but I knew it was difficult for her. If only I could make it all go away. Maybe I should give up the idea of being a missionary and take Pam back to the States where she wouldn't be so susceptible to illness. Whenever I suggested it, she argued that we were where God wanted us to be. This was confirmed one afternoon when we visited with our friend, Dolly Foster.

George and Dolly were not only our dearest friends at Betânia, they were also our neighbors, since our house was within walking distance from their center. One afternoon when Pam and I visited, Dolly was at their place alone. I always enjoyed walking into their small apartment because everything looked so American. A quilted spread covered their bed, and the bookshelves were overflowing with books. Family pictures were everywhere, and of course, there was George's recliner.

As soon as we sat down, Dolly said, "I've got something important to tell you. I was praying for you, and I felt like God gave me a word for you." She opened her Bible and read some verses aloud. It was a nice passage, but nothing particularly stood out to me.

Then she looked up, and tears were running down her cheeks. "He told me the reason you have to go through so much is that He is preparing you for wonderful things...He's planning these for you...." By now she was having trouble talking through her tears. I felt very touched and a little embarrassed by her love.

"Things are under control. He's taking care of you. He loves you in a special way, and so do we. It's all going to be okay." She wiped her eyes and tried to smile. Pam hugged her. How wonderful that God had given us friends such as George and Dolly! When we left that day, I was more impressed with Dolly's love for us than by what she had actually said. Later I would learn the significance of her words.

We didn't give up on being missionaries, and gradually Pam got better. Then she started having other symptoms. We went to the doctor, and this time there was great news...Pam was pregnant!

🙠 🙠 🙢 🙢

Marcelo was continuing to come up with ideas for new ways to present the gospel. I was so grateful that God had put us together as co-workers. One evening we were sitting together on the steps in front of our house.

"Jim," he pursed his lips and wrinkled his brow as he did in serious moments, "There's a winter festival every July in the city of Ouro Prêto. I think we should do an outreach there."

I had seen pictures of Ouro Prêto, an old colonial city two hours from Belo Horizonte. The architecture was kept as it had been during Portuguese rule. Marcelo explained that young people came from all over the country for the Ouro Prêto Winter Festival. There were artistic events, but the students came mostly to drink, party, and take drugs.

"It's a wild scene, but I think it would be a great chance to reach a lot of kids in one place," Marcelo said.

We prayed and talked it over and decided to do it.

The more we researched Ouro Prêto, the more fascinated I was by the challenge. The city had been built almost entirely by slaves. The Portuguese figured how long most slaves lived after starting hard labor and made advance orders for slaves to replace those who would die. Now Ouro Prêto was a city of 44,000, with limited evangelical witness. One small Baptist church served the entire town. The Methodists had a building, but only four women came to sporadic meetings.

I visited Ouro Prêto as part of our preparation. The white-plastered buildings with red-tiled roofs gleamed in the sunshine. Colorful flowers spilled over balconies and from window boxes. The winding streets were paved with cut stones. But Ouro Prêto's physical beauty dimmed as I remembered the suffering that went into building it. I thought I felt an oppressive spiritual atmosphere.

I knew the outreach was going to be really important. As usual, Marcelo had given us a great idea. So I wasn't prepared at all for the surprise I got when I came back to our house. One morning a knock came on our bedroom door. I opened it and found Marcelo. He looked very serious, maybe a little guilty. Then I saw his suitcase beside him. My stomach lurched a little. We went out to the front of the house and sat on the steps.

"I'm leaving."

I was numb with dismay and didn't know what to do. Should I try to talk him out of it? I wasn't sure.

"What made you decide this, Marcelo?"

"Being a missionary isn't the only way you can serve God. I'm going to get a job and help support you here."

I couldn't figure out any way to persuade him to stay. I felt more than a little rejected and didn't want to beg. Maybe this was best for him. Our work certainly wasn't very promising. I sat there without saying a word. Finally, Marcelo gathered his things and left.

His leaving was a major blow to the rest of our little group. Marcelo was a natural leader and many depended on his strength. Maybe others would leave. If more than two or three went, our mission might die before it got started. I didn't know what to do except pray. I asked God for His mercy and grace to help us. Marcelo was a very decisive guy, and I doubted he would return.

I was wrong. Four days later I was sitting on the front steps talking to some workers when Marcelo got off the bus. He walked toward us with his suitcase in his hand and a sheepish look on his face.

"Can I come back?"

"Sure, you can…. But I thought you were going to support missions financially."

"Well, I left here and headed downtown. I got off the bus, and as I was walking along, a man fell to the sidewalk in front of me. The man had dropped dead right there on the street! I felt the Spirit of the Lord say to me, 'You're not in My will, Marcelo. Death is unpredictable. It could happen to you anytime.' I was shaken but shrugged it off and went to a service last night at my church. A missionary was speaking. In the middle of his sermon, he stopped and said, 'I have a specific word for someone here tonight. You're thinking that you will support missions. But God has called you to be a missionary, not to support them. Don't flee the will of God in your life!' The next two days were miserable, and finally I just couldn't resist anymore. God has called me and won't let me get away from the call. I'm back to stay."

I smiled and clapped him on the back, and then everyone hugged him. As I turned to go inside, my shoulders felt lighter. The Lord had turned what could have been a decisive defeat—for Marcelo, for YWAM, and for me—into a victory.

ೋ ೋ ೋ ೋ

Our preparations for our outreach at Ouro Prêto continued with renewed vigor. By July we were ready. Through more miracles we were able to pay for our bus tickets. We climbed off the bus one cold, foggy morning in Ouro Prêto, hardly able to contain our excitement. Donning warm jackets and grabbing our suitcases, we walked toward the Methodist church, where we had arranged to stay in their basement.

As we walked, we saw lots of young people on the streets, including several long-haired, counterculture types. Everywhere we looked we saw people drinking, talking, and selling their beads and trinkets. It looked like San Francisco's Haight-Ashbury district in its hippie heyday, but set in the midst of seventeenth-century architecture. This would be interesting.

The Methodist basement was large enough to accommodate the girls on our team. Even though it smelled of mildew and the floorboards were rotting, it offered more privacy and was close to the bathroom. The guys would sleep in the sanctuary upstairs. Pam and I found a small basement room where we could lay our bedrolls. We borrowed a little stove and called it home. It wasn't much, but at least we had a place to retreat from the weather during the two weeks' outreach.

We were definitely a mixed group. About a third of our twenty had come off the streets. We had high hopes that they were truly converted, but only time would tell. Even we regular workers weren't exactly spiritual giants. In my more pessimistic moments, I wasn't sure who had more problems—the revelers who had come to party or the evangelists who had come to bring them the gospel.

As we went to share our faith on the streets, we found that everyone had come to have a good time. Finding new friends was a priority, so it was easy to start up conversations. The friendliness often changed, though, when they discovered why we were there and what we wanted to talk about. Since we were witnessing and preaching for hours every day, eventually lots of those who moved around the city had heard from us several times. Within a few days they were taunting us.

The weather was as cold as our reception, plus our bleak lodgings began to depress us. It wasn't supposed to be like this. The group was sinking into a pervasive gloom. We needed help.

One evening I gathered everyone in the basement for a meeting. The air was dank and stuffy. The humidity was so bad that moisture beaded on the walls, and it was cold. As I looked around the crowded room, I could see discouragement written on every face. No pep talk would work with this group.

I called on someone to lead us in worship. We started to sing rather woodenly. I was crying out to God inside. *How would we ever sustain this outreach? Was it worth sustaining?* Then something happened. I sensed that Jesus was with us in the basement. Shivers ran up and down my back.

People who had been staring blankly only moments before suddenly sat up, raised their hands, and spoke out with enthusiastic praises to God. Soon almost everyone was weeping and worshiping with abandon. Many fell to their knees, and others lay facedown on the floor. We lost track of time, and the hours advanced into the night. I felt wave after wave of joy wash over me. Jesus was so real I felt I could reach out and touch Him. It was as if we'd all been rescued from drowning in grimness. Everything in that dreary basement became beautiful.

At one point I glanced over at Graça, the Bible school student with all the problems. Her hands were raised, tears streamed down her cheeks, and she wore a look of transcendent joy. I'd never seen her like that. Jesus truly was in our midst.

TWELVE

"Go Away and Let Us Sin in Peace"

O U R attitudes the next morning were entirely different. During our private prayer hour, everyone seemed to be seeking God with renewed concentration. At breakfast, smiles were everywhere, and spontaneous praises sprinkled the conversation. During small group prayers, everyone was so eager that it was hard to get a turn to speak. Graça was telling everyone she had met Jesus for the first time the previous night.

We went into the streets with new spirit. We didn't have long to wait for our first dramatic breakthrough. One followed another, and another, and another. All of us had stories to tell when we reassembled that evening. Marcelo recounted a meeting with an American on the streets.

"His name was John, and he was from Oregon. He was hanging out with the drug users, and he was really hostile. He cut me off, growling that he didn't want any of this Jesus stuff. I found myself saying, 'You're going to see the hand of God in your life, John. You're going to be arrested.'"

As Marcelo finished his report, I thought that either he had gotten a direct word from God, or he was totally mixed up. The next evening I looked for Marcelo to learn if anything had happened with John. Marcelo said he and his partner had felt impressed to go to the jail that morning instead of into the streets.

"We thought we'd preach to the inmates. And you know who we saw as soon as we got to the cells? John! Although I had given him that word from God, I was surprised to see him in jail only one day later! I was worried he'd think I turned him into the police or something."

Marcelo slung his long hair off his face. "But he just said, 'Marcelo! I sent for you! Thanks for coming so quickly. Can you get me out of here?' I had a hard time convincing him that finding him there was a big surprise to me."

We didn't know how to help John with his legal problems or even if that was God's will. But the question was taken out of our hands when the police came to the Methodist church looking for Marcelo. They wanted his help. It appeared the local authorities were eager to find a way around enforcing their law on this young American. We negotiated John's release, assuming full responsibility for him. Shortly after John joined us, he turned his life over to Christ. We felt that this was one of many signs that God was blessing our evangelism in Ouro Prêto.

At dinner one night, a worker told about approaching a young man in the praça. "He began shouting that the winter festival used to be a great place to party, meet girls, and find drugs. But now every time he turned around someone was talking about God! He felt guilty about the things he came here to do. He said, 'Can't you go away and let us sin in peace?'"

We laughed. No, we were *not* going to let these people sin in peace! If they weren't going to submit to God, at least they would be aware of their sin before the winter festival was over.

By the end of our outreach, we believed more work should be done in Ouro Prêto. We rented a place for a team and appointed a young man named Jeriel and his sister, Célia, as leaders for the six who joined them. Jeriel set a goal to visit every house in Ouro Prêto within the next year.

We headed home to Belo Horizonte, taking John with us. He was leaving for the States in a few days. Our mission had been accomplished. Looking back on the outreach, I realized its significance: We now had two Brazilian YWAM operating locations!

❧ ❧ ❧ ❧

I visited our team in Ouro Prêto every week. One summer day as I approached the door, I could smell something burning. I hurried into the kitchen and saw a small pile of straw smoldering.

"Jeriel! What is this? Are you guys trying to fumigate?" Jeriel didn't say anything. In fact, everyone avoided my eyes. I waited for an explanation.

"We were trying to cook something to eat...."

"With straw?" I asked incredulously. "What's wrong with your stove?"

"We're out of gas."

Then I understood. "Jeriel, are you also out of money?"

"Yes, but we had enough to buy a little cornmeal."

Reluctantly they admitted that they hadn't eaten for three days. A lump came to my throat when I realized they were trying to cook the cornmeal in water. Fortunately, I had brought an offering with me from the base in Belo Horizonte. Someone ran off to the market, and we soon had a good meal cooking on the stove. Jeriel and the team were so happy. There's nothing like three days without eating to make people feel really good about food on the table. What touched me was that I didn't hear a single complaint from any of them. Their concerns were focused on reaching the people of Ouro Prêto.

When we were alone, I asked Jeriel how he coped with the pressure. Not only did he struggle with a lack of funds but also with a heavy schedule of ministry. He looked down and squirmed a little, like he didn't want to say.

"Well, I get up every morning at four o'clock," he explained. "If I spend at least three hours with the Lord before the day begins, I can make it."

I went home on the bus, worried about them, but fiercely proud of these humble, determined workers. How could anyone think Brazilian youth wouldn't choose to become missionaries? Was there anything they wouldn't do? I suggested to our people at Belo Horizonte that we pray more for the Ouro Prêto team and stepped up my visits.

Our work in Belo went on as before, but the victories seemed to be more frequent. We wanted to make a lasting impact on people, especially those the Church never seemed to touch. One Saturday I came home to find three of our team members kneeling in the dirt with someone. They were hovering around him, praying in loud voices with their eyes squeezed shut. I looked at the young man, a thin black with a big Afro hairstyle. He was a definite contrast to our guys as he bowed quietly in the middle of all the energetic praying. He wore skimpy white shorts and a T-shirt.

I asked Pam who he was; she explained that Elisa, one of our girls, had talked to him about the Lord. His name was Rui, and he'd come to find out more about the gospel. I looked outside at the knot of workers still pouring loud prayers over Rui's bowed head. If he ever escaped this, he'd probably never come back. A couple of minutes later, I saw him jump on his ten-speed bike and pedal quickly away.

Rui did come back, though. This time I was there, and it was Sunday. I took him with me for the half-mile walk to Betânia's church. We talked about the Lord all the way. He bobbed along, full of nervous energy and intellectual arguments. As we walked into church, I was aware again of his rather far-out appearance. Besides the oversized hairstyle, he was wearing tight red pants. I wasn't sure how this would be received by the eighty people sitting on the wooden pews waiting for the service to start.

As it turned out, Rui was the one who felt uncomfortable. We found a seat just as the singing began. He winced as momentum built.

"This is no place for me," he whispered hoarsely. "These people are pure, and I'm filthy. I've got to get out of here!" He looked agitated, and he twisted and turned as if he were about to burst.

"Sure, man," I said. "Let's go outside." I took him by the arm, and we walked out into the heat of the bright sunshine. He calmed down a bit when we got away from the singing. Still, he was obviously nervous. "Can I pray for you, Rui?"

"I guess so." His breath was uneven.

I placed my hand on his shoulder and closed my eyes. "Father, Rui has a need. He's not feeling well, being close to Your people. He can see how filthy he is inside, and it makes him want to get away from here. Lord, come down and free him from this anxiety. Bring calm to his…"

Suddenly Rui's shoulder wasn't under my hand anymore, then I heard a thud. I opened my eyes and Rui was flat on his back, his eyes closed. I sat in the red dust beside him and continued praying. He finally sat up, blinking, and I took him back inside the church.

Something changed in Rui that day. He could no longer get away from the Lord's dealings, and within a few weeks he was well converted. He brought his wife, Marilac, to meet us. She was pretty in her long, flowing hippie dress. Rui told us proudly that she was expecting their baby. Marilac was skeptical about Rui's newfound faith, although by now he had persuaded several people to accept Christ.

THIRTEEN

Small Miracles

P A M ' S pregnancy wasn't going well.

Only four months along, she was having strong contractions on a regular basis. Her doctor told us not to worry; he said some women have contractions throughout pregnancy. But then, during one of Pam's visits to the doctor, she experienced a series of pains while she was on the examination table. He seemed surprised at their severity.

"It's too early for this. We're going to have to do something about it."

I breathed a sigh of relief. At least he was taking us seriously. The "something" we had to do soon was a difficult prescription. He gave Pam muscle relaxants, and then he told her to stay in bed for the last five months of her pregnancy.

We went back to our room at the YWAM house. These four walls would be Pam's world for the next several months. The problem was, when she wasn't experiencing the pains, she felt normal. Still, we decided we would follow the doctor's orders to the letter. This baby was too important to us to take any chances.

One day during her sixth month, Pam called me into the room. "Jim, the contractions are harder and closer together. I've timed them and they're only five minutes apart. You'd better call Dr. Daniel." She gasped as another contraction gripped her.

The doctor told me to bring her in immediately, adding, "You must understand that the baby is too small. We won't be able to save it."

I went back to Pam and reported the conversation, leaving out the part about losing the baby. It was a terrible secret, and my heart felt like lead. I walked quickly to Betânia to borrow a car, my mind in turmoil. "Lord," I prayed, "I don't understand. Why is it so hard to do Your will? We've done our best to follow You. Why should our lives be full of need and hardship? We can't even seem to have a baby. Why don't You help us?"

I was in no condition to hear His still, small voice. I didn't take time to listen for it. At any rate, no answer came. I got the car and went to take my wife to the hospital and face the loss of our first child.

However, when I walked into our room and saw Pam lying in bed, something inside me rebelled against the whole situation. It filled me with anger. This was not going to happen! I knelt down beside the bed and began to pray, but it was no nice little prayer. It was more like pouring rage over the unseen world. I laid my hand on Pam's abdomen. It seemed as if it wasn't quite as hard as it had been. Another contraction took hold. I prayed fervently. Another one came, but it was quite a few minutes later.

"Pammie, isn't it getting better?"

"Yes, I think so. The contractions seem to be getting weaker."

Eventually they subsided, and my anger gradually turned to worship. I don't know how much time passed before we agreed that things were back within non-crisis limits. I called the doctor, told him we wouldn't be coming, and returned the car to Betânia.

At Pam's insistence, I continued to make my weekly bus trips to Ouro Prêto. I felt so torn between wanting to be by her side to help pass the endlessly long days and wanting to continue our work with the Brazilians. Often as the bus passed the river that flows through Belo Horizonte, I would look at the clusters of tin and cardboard shanties on the banks. With all our difficulties, we still lived like royalty compared to these people. "Someday, Lord, help us to help them, too," I prayed.

A major surprise awaited me on one of my trips to our Ouro Prêto headquarters. Célia met me at the door with two tiny black girls hiding behind her skirts, peeking around at me with large eyes. "Célia," I teased, "you didn't tell me you were expecting any additions!" She laughed and waved me into their living room. Soon we were joined by her brother, Jeriel, and the rest of the team.

"So, where did you get these two cuties?"

Jeriel nodded to his sister. "Tell him, Célia."

"Remember we were going door to door, trying to reach every house in Ouro Prêto?" I nodded, still trying to get a clear look at the little girls hiding in her skirts. One looked about five years old; the other, three. Célia said she and another girl had gone to a remote area out of town. When they clapped in front of a solitary mud hut, there was no answer. They started to leave when they heard a whimper. They knew they had to get inside the house, and they resorted to breaking through a badly fastened shutter. What they found was shocking and sad.

"These two little things were in there all alone," recounted Célia. "The smell was the first thing that hit us. Over in the corner, we saw the pile of human waste…that was where they'd been using the bathroom. Who knows how long they had been locked in there? They cried pitifully, like kittens, covered with sores and filth, with their hair matted."

I looked at their shiny faces. Both little girls had barrettes holding back masses of curly hair.

"Where were their parents?" I asked angrily.

"We didn't know at first. We looked around, and the only food we found was chunks of old, dried bread. They had been drinking out of an aluminum basin half full of water. We bought some food and tried to clean them up. Then we waited for their father. It was three days before he returned."

The man was surly and unrepentant. His wife had left, so whenever he went on a drinking spree, he locked up his daughters. "He told us he didn't want them, and if we were so concerned, we could take them ourselves," said Célia. "And so we did."

When Célia finished the story, the whole team looked at me expectantly.

It was 1977, and I knew of no such children's ministries in YWAM anywhere in the world at that time. I didn't know if we were supposed to get involved in such projects, or if we were to stick exclusively to evangelism and training. We prayed about it and discussed our options. I asked the team if they had thought about the extra needs of children—milk, clothing, and eventually, even school supplies. After all, this was the team I had found cooking cornmeal on a straw fire not very long ago.

They assured me that they could trust the Lord to provide for the girls, too. We decided we had to care for these two children. If we had the same spirit as Christ, we couldn't refuse a need like this one. Our obedience to God's call to evangelism had brought the need to our attention.

This was only the beginning. Shortly afterward, the Ouro Prêto team took in a boy on the brink of starvation. Although the doctor said he was too far gone to save, the team prayed for him and nursed him back to health. Within a few months, they had taken in even more children. But the team never went hungry anymore. Somehow, there was always enough to feed everyone and provide milk and other extras for all the children.

Pam continued to stay in bed, but by the time January rolled around, even though she was still pregnant, she was able to move to another Bible school. This would be our second summer program. It was a crazy day when we relocated to the school, and I was thankful for the friends who helped us. One newcomer was a silent, athletic-looking young man named Paulo Sergio.

"Paulo is a friend of Marcelo's," someone explained. "He's from Campos." I shook his hand. He had a firm grip but was unshaven and smelled of cigarettes.

"Hello. I've come for the summer program," he said. I had to wonder if he was ready for missionary training. He assured me that he was, and he proved it during the following weeks. I was wrong to have misgivings; he was a serious student and fit in well with our thirty-five participants. During the school he surrendered to Christ and was finally free of his bad habits.

One day near the end of the month, Rui brought his wife, Marilac, to a few classes. She hadn't given her life to Jesus yet. We guessed that she had seen Rui excited about new philosophies before and hesitated to embrace another. I wondered why she'd taken the trouble to come. She was hugely pregnant now, like Pam, and soon they were chatting about the common trials of pregnancy.

Wedge and Shirley were with us again, and that afternoon Wedge preached about the power of God to free us from our past. When we started praying, many displayed great emotion, bursting into tears and loud prayers, confessing bondages of their lives. Marilac watched with round eyes. After it was over she declared her intention to follow Jesus.

On February 3, 1977, the day after Wedge and Shirley left, Pam gave birth to a girl. Although our daughter was bald, in my impartial opinion she was exceptionally beautiful, unusually alert, and intelligent. A strong, protective feeling swelled in my chest, and I looked up and down the hospital corridor, almost hoping something threatening would appear so I could protect my little girl. I nestled her on my arm and whispered thanks to God. She was a breathing miracle. We named her Vanya.

❧ ❧ ❧ ❧

New challenges were on the horizon. The team in Ouro Prêto now had 11 children living with them. The landlord wanted them to move. Because they had visited every home in the city, they felt their work in Ouro Prêto was over for now, and they moved back to Belo Horizonte. Of course, they brought the children with them—they were our permanent commitment.

It was wonderful to have them all with us, but space was becoming a problem. We had already been playing a kind of musical chairs with forty full-time staff in our rented house. We had to keep a certain number out traveling, ministering in churches at all times. If they all came home at once, we wouldn't have a place for everyone to sleep. As it was, some were sleeping in the kitchen and living room.

I had to find another place, but where?

Then I heard that the mission located in the L-shaped building was vacant. This was the facility Pam and I had visited as guests of the missionary from New Zealand shortly after we arrived in Brazil. It could accommodate a hundred people if we really stacked them in. I smiled as I remembered wondering if we could ever fill such a place.

I went to talk to the owners of the building—another mission organization. My hopes died. They didn't want to rent. They wanted to sell...for $300,000. I knew anything was possible with God, but maybe not with us, not yet.

The World Cup soccer games were coming up soon in Argentina. Loren Cunningham came to Brazil and challenged us to use the event to mobilize more Brazilians. Like everywhere else in South America, soccer was a passion in Brazil.

We planned seminars in seven major cities around Brazil to train volunteers for the World Cup outreach. This brought up a real need. It was becoming more and more difficult to take the bus everywhere we went. In fact, with the schedule we had planned in those seven cities, we desperately needed a vehicle of our own.

Larry Darby, our friend from Betânia Bible School, gave us an offering to buy a vehicle. I immediately started shopping. The only van available in Brazil was the Volkswagen. I must have looked at ten, but those in our price range were rolling wrecks. Then I answered an ad in the newspaper and found a one-owner van. The man had obviously taken good care of it—it was in great condition. It was blue and only four years old. There was one problem: It cost several hundred dollars more than we had.

The next morning we gathered in our room and prayed. It was impossible, but it seemed as though God was saying that the blue van was for us. In the middle of our prayer meeting, a shadow fell across the living room. I looked up, and there was George Foster filling the front door. He pulled something out of his pocket and tossed it across the room to me. It was a fat brick of Brazilian currency, securely wrapped with rubber bands.

"That's to help with your new vehicle," he said.

I did a quick count, and it was just what we needed. We all jumped around, praised God, and thanked George. What friends we had! What a God we served! Later that day we went out and closed the deal on the van. Now we had a dependable vehicle to make the trip to do the seminars in seven cities. We could go in our own car!

❧ ❧ ❧ ❧

We were about to leave on our seven-city tour. It was March of 1978, and a small team would take the trip. Gerson, our old friend and new colleague, and I would do most of the teaching. Pam and our baby, Vanya, would go as well, along with two other team members. Excitement was high as we made rapid preparations.

A few days before we were to leave, I pulled our fine, blue VW van into our garage, happy to have something to park in it. As I got out I felt uneasy. I didn't know why, but I had a compulsion to bend down and look under the van. I felt silly and tried to dismiss it, but the feeling got stronger. Finally, just to get rid of the compulsion, I looked.

What I saw chilled me. Underneath, a clear liquid dripped from the engine compartment. What was that? It couldn't be water—the engine was air cooled. I walked around to where the leak was, put my hand under the drip, then smelled it. It was gasoline! Quickly the realization settled on me. The gas tank on those vans sat right in the engine compartment, with the electrical parts nearby. I'd seen many such vans in the middle of the street on fire. Then I remembered.

At our first training program that prayer group of new students had prayed for a vehicle. They'd claimed to see a blue van. A girl had seen a vision of it on fire in the middle of the street, and they had prayed it wouldn't happen. At the time I thought it was a weird prayer—the naive students hadn't learned how to hear the voice of God yet. Now I felt a charge of excitement go through me as I realized that my compulsion to look under the van was an answer to prayers from two years before!

The next day we pulled out the engine and found our gas tank had developed a hole in the bottom. Gas was puddling there before running off and dripping to the ground. Our car was a rolling fire bomb. Thank God for weird prayers!

We worked long hours and had a new tank in the van in time for our seven-city tour. As a result of the tour, 120 Brazilians went to the outreach in Argentina. One young Brazilian left from the World Cup outreach to work with YWAM in Japan. I hoped he would be a seed planted for the future. Maybe someday we'd send hundreds of Brazilians all over the world.

After the Argentina outreach, Gerson stayed on with us. A number of other Brazilians also wanted to join our work in Belo Horizonte. We were gaining momentum now, but where would we put these extra workers? I thought of our rented house and shuddered. Crowding any more people into that facility was physically impossible. Besides, we needed a place where we could conduct longer training programs than in the borrowed Bible schools during summer.

I searched for property. Nothing we could afford was large enough. The L-shaped building kept coming to my mind. I prayed again and thought the Lord said that building was for us. "How can that be, Lord?" I asked. "We have a terrible time just coming up with the few hundred dollars we need for food and rent for our little place. How could we handle that amount?"

The thought came to open my Bible. I did and my eyes fell on Deuteronomy 7:22. It was about the children of Israel going into the Promised Land. God promised to give them the land a little at a time so that the animals of prey wouldn't overcome them. God was saying something, but I didn't understand. "What does this mean, Lord? Will You give us the mission building a little at a time?" It didn't make sense. They wanted a full cash payment. Because of hyperinflation, Brazilian banks didn't finance this sort of thing. As for renting, the owners already said they weren't interested.

"What are You saying, God?"

He didn't answer, but I decided to approach the mission again about renting, although they had refused before.

To my surprise, they agreed. The only drawback was, they wanted $1,200 a month—a huge sum for us! I consulted with other Christian leaders and with our staff. We prayed intensely and decided to go ahead. Renting seemed to be what God meant when He said He would give it to us little by little. I signed the contract, and on July 12, 1978, we moved in.

We somehow came up with the first month's rent, and contrary to Brazilian custom, paid in advance. By August, our first five-month school started, full and bustling. One morning as the seventy students gathered for class in the large dining room, I looked around and thought, *What a God we serve!* This was the very place where the missionary from New Zealand and his wife had entertained us during our first days in Brazil. I had wondered that night if we would ever have enough workers to fill such a place. Now three years later, here we were! I hadn't been aware of any dramatic victories or stunning tactical moves. The only possible explanation was that God had done it. We were still a motley crew. We were just a larger one now.

We were going on with new ministry initiatives as well. We'd sent a team to start a new base of operations in Pôrto Alegre, in the southernmost state of Brazil. Rui and Marilac went along to help. Some Christians in Pôrto Alegre promised to pay the team's rent for the first year! I only wished I knew how we were going to pay next month's rent here in Belo.

Then one day everything went wrong.

FOURTEEN

Pressed in on All Sides

W E had been barely surviving since moving into the L-shaped building. Somehow each month we had squeaked through on unexpected offerings to make our rent payments. We gave up meat, getting by on rice and *angu*, a cornmeal mush boiled until it was solid.

But then even frugality failed. The fourth month's rent was due, and we had big problems. Hardly any money had come in. We only had half the rent. We explained to the owners, and they agreed to wait two weeks for the second half of the payment.

Now the two weeks' grace was up. Two days from now I had to pay another $600. And after breakfast tomorrow, we would be out of food.

I sat in my office, fighting to keep a positive attitude. What were we going to do? We were feeding more than one hundred people, including eleven homeless children. How could I face them and say we didn't have money for food? Or for rent? I didn't think it could get any worse.

A knock came at the door.

"Jim! Pam says to come quickly. She needs you!"

Pam was pregnant again, and we hoped it would be easier this time. I ran to our apartment and found her lying on the bed.

"It's the baby, Jim," she explained between winces. "It's just like last time." The contractions were coming hard and fast, and it was still five months before her due date. We rushed her to the doctor, and a while later she was back in our room, hooked to an IV dripping muscle relaxant into her veins. The doctor ordered bed rest for the remainder of her pregnancy.

I trudged back to my little office. Complete bed rest? In two days, we might not have a roof over our heads! I closed my office door behind me and locked it. The room was bare except for a table and a straight-backed wooden chair. The large window had no curtains. I sat on the chair, folded my arms on the table, and put my head down.

"God, I'm so tired and worried and mad! What are we going to do?"

A knock came at the door. I ignored it. I had to pray. I didn't want to see anyone. Not now. Another knock, more insistent. I held my breath, hoping whoever it was would go away. Then he, or she, started pounding.

"Jim! Jim!"

It was Marcelo. I knew he had been under a lot of pressure lately. His wife was pregnant again, only months after giving birth to their little girl, and they were having money problems, too. I didn't know how to help. He was the last person I wanted to see today. I didn't answer. Maybe if I kept really quiet he'd understand that I was in prayer. Within a few minutes I heard something at the window behind me. Marcelo was peering in with his hands cupped around his eyes. Good grief! He was more stubborn than I! I struggled with the sliding window until I got it open.

"Jim," he said with worry wrinkling his brow, "I bumped into our old landlord downtown today. He has decided to sell and wants his house just like new. He's going to strip the plaster off and redo it, and refinish the doors, doorframes, moldings, window frames, and hardwood floors."

"We painted and cleaned before we left," I said, confused. "What does this have to do with us?"

"He wants to repaint the entire house inside and out with better paint. He says since we were the last tenants, we should pay for the whole job. Here's the estimate." He handed me a sheet of paper. I looked at the bottom figure, trying to convert the value into dollars. It came to more than $3,000. I closed the window. Now what? Trouble was piling on top of trouble, and I couldn't even get away to pray!

I noticed a small door in the wall of my office. It was a storage space under the stairway. Here was a place no one could find me! I clutched my Portuguese Bible and crawled through the two-foot-high opening. It was cramped, dusty, and dark. I pulled the door shut and began to cry out to God.

"Lord, this is terrible! I don't understand. I have friends who don't even try to please You. They were called to missions, too, but they never followed the call. Now they have homes and families. They pay their bills. Their lives are so manageable. We, on the other hand, are always on the brink of disaster. People think we're irresponsible and crazy. Even our friends don't think we're very smart. You never ask us to do anything but the impossible. We don't have enough food to eat. And Pam and I can't even have a baby without terrible struggle."

I waited, breathing the musty air, but there was only silence in the space under the stairs. "Why is it so hard, God? What's happening with us? Am I destined to lead all these people into disaster? How can I fulfill my responsibilities when I have nowhere to turn? Has Your hand lifted from this ministry? Is that why we can't pay the rent? Are we supposed to close everything and do something else?"

Jim, turn to Jeremiah 12:5.

I cracked the door to let in some light and opened my Bible, fully expecting a word of encouragement. When I found and read the Scripture, though, I was at a loss. How was I to interpret these words? I read:

If you have raced with men on foot and they have worn you out, how can you compete with horses? If you stumble in a safe country, how will you manage in the thickets by the Jordan?

"Lord, do You mean to say all of this is just the foot soldiers? Is the cavalry about to come over the hill? Do You mean it's going to get worse?"

No more answers came.

Wasn't that just like God? I never could get Him to talk when I wanted Him to, or to obey my wishes. Then when He did speak, He told me to do something impossible. I had never been able to "confess" or "positive think" Him into submission. I sighed and crawled out through the small door, feeling chastised and a little foolish. I was still worried, but I brushed the dust off my clothes, unlocked the door to my office, and resolved to face whatever was coming.

The next morning I gathered Marcelo, Gerson, Jaime, Paulo Sergio, and our other stalwarts. I told them the situation. We prayed, and someone felt we were to go to two of our friends in the city and tell them of our need. We'd never done anything like that before because we had always prided ourselves on only sharing our needs with God. The thought of telling anyone else seemed uncomfortable. However, the more we prayed, the more we felt that leading. We decided the plan was God's.

When we finished our prayers, it was time for our morning discipleship class. Also, the cooks were arriving in the kitchen to prepare lunch. The noon meal is the biggest of the day in Brazil, and they usually start work at 9 a.m. I hadn't told them about our predicament, and so they looked puzzled as I hurried by. I knew what was going through their minds: Why hadn't anyone gone shopping for food? I went into the classroom and started teaching.

A half hour later I heard gravel crunching in our driveway. I glanced out the window. It was Larry Darby in his green Chevrolet pickup. I gave a break to the students and went out to greet him, wondering why he had come. He had recently convinced me that I should take up jogging, but with all our problems I had skipped it for a couple of days. I hoped he wouldn't ask. He didn't.

"I was at the wholesale outlet, shopping for our school," he explained. "How are things with you guys?"

"Okay," I fibbed. "We're doing all right."

He smiled. "I hope you don't mind what I've done. While I was shopping I felt I should get a few staples for your kitchen. They're in the back of the pickup. Can you use them?"

The back of the Chevy was heaped with food. Bags of rice, beans, and potatoes were there, along with "luxuries" we hadn't been able to buy for a long time—fresh fruit, vegetables, and a case of eggs. Could we use them? Of course! We were going to have lunch! God had come through again.

When we told our two friends in the city of our need, they helped, and we were able to pay the rent on Friday, leaving two weeks to pay $1,200 for the next month. Then our former landlord agreed to let us do the work on his house ourselves, which meant we only had to pay for the materials.

We ate mostly cornmeal that month and sold our refrigerator to help pay for the renovation materials. It seemed so unfair to have to refurbish his house. And, when we finished, he even charged us rent for the month we worked on it! I struggled with the situation, but I felt it wasn't right to take him to court, so we paid what he asked.

Marcelo's situation worsened. His wife gave birth to twins, and while that was exciting, it put more pressure on him. Now he had three children born in one calendar year. They didn't have adequate missions support, and money was a constant worry. He was such a valuable member of our team, but I wasn't sure how long he could continue to bear the stress.

By this time our ministry had become very busy. We had an orphanage, our street evangelism ministry, and traveling teams speaking in churches. We also were doing our first full-length Discipleship Training School. Even though our future seemed in doubt, we explored new ministry opportunities.

One idea was to have a special outreach in Rio de Janeiro during the annual spiritist celebration. From our first days in Brazil, Pam and I had heard about this event on the beaches of Rio. It happened every New Year's Eve, as a million spiritists came to worship their goddess of the seas, Iemanjá. It was a spiritual, cultural, and media event, capturing the imagination of the entire nation. From what we gleaned from the television coverage, the event was demonic, with spirits entering thousands, causing them to fall and writhe and cry out in strange voices.

Should we go into such a gathering? With so many spirit mediums in one place, what if we loosed more demons than we could bind? Most of the Christians in Rio wouldn't let their members go near the beaches on New Year's Eve. And to make matters worse, I couldn't go myself. Pam had nearly lost our second child several times and was confined to bed. I finally decided to send fifteen of our most seasoned workers. I hoped I wasn't making a mistake.

FIFTEEN

The Promised Land

T H E report from Rio was positive. Our band of fifteen reached many who were on the beaches more out of curiosity than anything else. No major disasters occurred, and the presence of a few Christians seemed to make a dent in the darkness. Based on their report we started to pray that God would replace that pagan festival with a Christian celebration. I don't know if we believed our prayer could be answered, but we knew we had to try.

In the meantime, our battle for survival continued. I was still waiting for the cavalry to come riding over the hill. It wasn't a long wait. What should have been one of the happiest days of my life was tainted by more bad news.

Just after midnight, March 3, 1979, our second child was born—a boy! Jonathan James was healthy, Pam's ordeal was over, and I was ecstatic as I arrived home from the all-night vigil. I showered, changed clothes, and napped for a few hours. Over breakfast I told Vanya she had a new baby brother. She frowned, puzzling over what that was. I was about to return to Pam in the hospital when the phone rang.

"Jim? This is Douglas. Our directors have met, and we decided we don't want to rent the property anymore. We want to sell it, and we wanted you to know right away, since we're giving you first option to buy."

My mind raced to take in the news. Douglas was the representative of the mission that rented us the L-shaped building. As he talked, my mind flashed to the Scripture God had given me under the stairs. It seemed I could hear the drumming of the horses' hooves in Jeremiah 12:5. What would we do now?

Next came the details: The asking price was $300,000; if we decided not to buy, we would have to vacate the property by July 12, slightly more than four months away; our special price would be "only" $280,000. I put down the phone. My euphoria over my son's birth was gone. Could we come up with $280,000? It was so far beyond us that it was laughable. I knew the limits of our options. Our budget couldn't handle the cost on any property large enough to accommodate ninety-six staff and students plus the eleven children in our orphanage. We had exactly nineteen weeks until we were out on the street. I knew God could easily come up with the necessary money to buy the place if it was His will. That was the key: We needed to know His will for us.

I called for a special week of prayer and fasting with our workers. One morning I gathered Pam, Marcelo, Jaime, Paulo, Gerson, and several others into my office to pray.

"We've got to hear from God," I announced. I told them we could no longer rent our building, and previous searches for property had been fruitless. Now we had a July deadline to move unless we bought this place. "I know God could give us this building, but I'm not sure that's what He wants for us. We need to hear from Him."

We began to pray, huddled in my office, waiting for God to speak to each one. After minutes of silence, I began to poll them. "What did you get from God?" I asked. "Who wants to share first?"

"This Scripture reference came into my mind," replied a young worker. "It's in Jeremiah 32, about buying property."

A woman spoke up from across the room. "Maybe that's what my Scripture meant. I thought I should read Genesis 23, but it was about Abraham buying a burial plot for Sarah. It didn't make any sense at first. Unless God is saying something about buying land."

Then a recruit from southern Brazil said, "You know what I just remembered? A few weeks ago in church, a woman came up to me and said that God told her we were going to build ourselves a house. I thought she was confused because YWAMers don't build houses, do they?" His blue eyes were wide with questions.

One by one, we shared our impressions. Someone had been led to a Scripture about laying a foundation and raising walls. Everyone in the circle felt we were to buy land and to build something. Everyone except Marcelo. He had received a verse about not entering the land. I looked at him and felt a pang of sadness. Why was Marcelo's word different from the others? He knew how to hear from the Lord as well as anyone. I feared that this was a sign that Marcelo would leave us, his ministry taking him in a different direction.

Eleven of us believed God was leading us to buy land and build something. That guidance was clear. As the special week of prayer continued, our conviction grew. I remembered the word about the horsemen and wondered if God knew we would need strong guidance to withstand the battles ahead. We started to look for land.

Marcelo and I and two others went to see Décio Camargo, a local Presbyterian who dealt in real estate. I had only met Décio briefly and was a bit nervous when we clapped our hands at the front gate before his substantial-looking house. Décio came out, greeted us warmly, and invited us in. He was a frail little man, dressed in old gray slacks and a white cotton shirt with the sleeves rolled up. His simple, straightforward manner put us at ease. Taking my arm, he led us across a patio and into a cramped room he used as his office. It was lined with shelves heaped with files and loose papers. We sat down and faced him across his cluttered desk. I explained our situation, and he asked some questions. Then he grew quiet as he thought about it.

"How much money do you have?" he finally asked.

"We have only our trust in God, Décio. We don't really know what to do, but we think building is the answer. We need a place."

"How much money do you think you can raise by July?"

"We don't have any experience in fund-raising," I replied. "I wouldn't know how to start doing that."

Our exchange brought a long period of silence. He stared at some invisible point in space and drummed his fingers on the desk. Finally he spoke. "I've helped a lot of ministries over the years, and I'd like to help you. I think I might have a deal I can offer you."

He joined us in our blue van and directed us to a property quite a distance from town. We jolted over rough dirt roads until we finally stopped where the road stopped, at the top of a hill. By now it was early evening, but we could see in the fading light a narrow corridor of raw, red dirt, gouged out of the native brush by a bulldozer. Rain had washed away much of it, leaving deep crevasses and gullies. If we went any farther, we would have to get out and walk.

Décio explained that he was suffering from advanced diabetes and couldn't see very well. He gestured vaguely toward the hilly countryside and said, "It's over there somewhere. There's no electricity or water. This is the only road, and the nearest bus line is quite a distance away. There aren't any buildings, but I think we might be able to work out something, if you're interested."

The next morning we went back on our own. We carefully made our way down the semi-road for as far as we could in the van until we got stuck in a mudhole, then we walked the rest of the way. On one side of the property, we found a pond beside a nice grove of trees. But the land was so overgrown that we couldn't get in without a machete. The living wall was penetrated only by a narrow trail, probably worn by fishermen over the years.

We talked it over, standing there in the strong midmorning sunshine. It would be a difficult site to build anything on. Especially since none of us had any building experience. It would take a lot of earth-moving just to get a level place for a foundation. That would take time, and our July deadline was only seventeen weeks away. Besides, how could we manage without electricity? Where would we get water? And how could we run schools without a bus line for people to come and go?

None of the guys felt this was the place. But something in me said, *Yes, this is right.* Even though it would be difficult, the hillside would someday make it a more interesting location. However, we decided to visit other realtors to see what else was available.

I had to travel for a couple of weeks, visiting the Pôrto Alegre base and speaking at some conferences. I was glad to go. Contacting real estate offices and bargaining over land without a penny in our pockets didn't seem like fun.

When I returned, we talked over the possibilities. Marcelo, Gerson, and the others had found some nice places, but they all sold on a cash basis. Inflation was about sixty percent a year, so it was impossible to get long-term loans. We didn't have the money to buy anything. However, we knew God could do a miracle and give us any piece of land we had seen. We continued praying. As the days sped by, though, we all began to feel more and more guided to Décio's property. We went to see him again.

"I think I can help you," he said, hobbling over to his cluttered desk and sitting down. He scribbled a figure on a piece of paper and handed it to me. I made a rapid conversion to dollars in my head—he was ask-ing $25,000. "You wouldn't have to start paying until a year from now. That way you can put your money into building. After twelve months, you can give me monthly payments."

As I digested this welcomed information, he dug through over-stuffed files, explaining that the property wasn't just his. It also belonged to seven of his brothers and sisters. I got the feeling that if it were all his, he would have given it to us.

By early April we finalized the agreement, allowing us to start working immediately. Décio donated his share of the payment, as did one of his sisters. Also, with sixty percent annual inflation, they were all making a substantial gift by agreeing to the long-term repayment. I was humbled by this man, his family, and their generosity.

With that agreement in hand, we went to the mission we were renting from and asked for consideration on the rent. They were using the money for their own expenses, but they graciously agreed to stretch it out for us. We would pay half the normal rent until we moved, then continue four more months, making up the full amount.

God had opened another door for us. Now we needed the strength, faith, and skill to walk through it. We hurried home to announce our good news to our staff and students.

SIXTEEN

Picks, Hoes, and Heavy Sacks

W E ' L L start our building program at once," I explained after the cheers had died down. "But first we'll have to clear the land. It's overgrown and hilly, and we'll all have to pitch in to get it ready, then we'll lay our first foundation."

I looked around at the ninety-six faces turned toward me. Some were newcomers off the streets; others were fresh out of churches and eager to serve Jesus. Our seasoned staff, more aware than the novices of what we were proposing, looked serious. A young man spoke up. "What if some of us don't know anything about construction?"

I glanced over at Gerson and saw his wry smile. He was sitting by his bride, Elisa, a quiet Argentine girl. "Uh…actually, most of us are in that position. But we'll learn fast, won't we?" I laughed. "Does *anyone* have any building experience?"

A short, plump guy in the back spoke up. "I worked in a coffin factory for a while." Now everyone joined in the laughter.

As the discussion continued, I looked around the room. Several were from that first group—the students who had met me as I lay wheezing with pneumonia. There was Graça, the girl Larry had apologized for leaving with us. Ever since the Spirit's outpouring in Ouro Prêto, she had been a different person and an effective evangelist. Down from her sat Jaime Araújo, the skinny kid with glasses who had turned out to be an intelligent, energetic man of God—a real leader. He was responsible for much of our administration and knew the financial situation. He wore a sober expression. Marcelo sat with his arms folded, looking as though he'd swallowed something sour. He wasn't in favor of what we were doing because of the guidance he'd gotten during our early prayer session.

All in all, it was a good group, and, except for another American couple and a couple of Argentines, all were Brazilian. A warmth welled up in me. Nothing could be more important than this. No matter what lay ahead, it would be worth it if these and others like them could be a part of reaching the whole world with the gospel.

Gradually the discussion slowed and I reminded them, "We have fewer than three months before we need to move from here. But I believe we can get something built to live in before that." I outlined a daily schedule—rising at five in the morning and working until six in the evening. Then we'd return to do our classes at night, extending them over six months. Instead of doing a mission field trip after the classroom phase, we would do construction.

"Excuse me, Jim," said one of the younger guys, a newly arrived student. "Can we vote on whether or not to do this?"

It took me back a second, but then everyone laughed, and that answered his question. Actually, we had no alternative. This meant survival for YWAM in Brazil. We also knew we didn't have the finances to do what we were proposing, so before the meeting closed we decided to hold on to God with all the intensity we could muster. Among other strategies, we inaugurated a twenty-four-hour prayer vigil until July.

Things were getting more and more impossible. I was beginning to suspect God liked it that way. I didn't. A crew of eight tackled the job of digging a well and clearing the brush for the initial survey of the property lines.

It was fun for the first day or two, carving a perfectly round hole in the moist, yielding dirt. Then we hit the water table. From then on I spent days stuck up to my knees in mud at the bottom of a shaft with a diameter of about thirty-two inches. It was almost too tight to move in the tiny space, let alone manipulate tools to get the job done.

At this point we needed to slide concrete sleeves down as we went so the sides of the well wouldn't cave in. Sometimes it took an hour or two to get a sleeve down ten inches into the sticky mud. Two of us traded off digging and hauling the buckets of mud up with a rope. As I watched the heavy bucket swaying directly over my head, I wondered if the flimsy handle would give way and the bucket come hurtling down at me. It would split my skull open, but we had no money to buy hard hats.

Every day our clothes were covered with mud and grit. Even though this was fall in the Southern Hemisphere, by noon the tropical sun turned the moisture in our clothes to steam. My feet, always my greatest weakness, hurt with every step. After a week, we were finally finished digging the well. It felt so good to arrive the next day in the early morning chill, unroll a rope, tie it to a new black bucket, and lower it. When it came up full of crystal-clear water we cheered. We all had cups—that must have been the sweetest water any of us had ever tasted.

We also built a square room from homemade gray bricks with mud for mortar. It was about eight by ten feet and provided accommodations so that two guys could guard our picks, shovels, hoes, and building materials each night. That would allow us to store enough tools on the premises to put everyone to work.

We established a routine: We dragged ourselves out of bed at five each morning to spend some time with the Lord; then after a light breakfast of bread and coffee, we left at seven to walk two and a half miles to the building site. Upon arrival we met and prayed for fifteen minutes. By 8:15 we were all at our places working. Outhouses had to be dug and constructed. Land had to be cleared so we could select building sites. Everyone was working hard with enthusiasm and high-spirited competition. Shortly after noon the blue van would arrive with lunch. Quitting time was 6 p.m., when we trudged home with lots of blisters and sore muscles. No one complained, though, and only a few fell asleep during class each night.

After a few days we had the place marked for our first building where we could live barracks-style until we built more structures. It would be a long, one-story building with men on one end, women on the other, and a few individual rooms in the middle for married couples. But first, we had to level the site. We didn't have money to rent a bulldozer, so we had to clear it by hand.

One day Décio came by to see how things were going. His jaw dropped. "Wow, this looks like Bible times!" The only biblical parallel I could think of was the Israelites' slavery in Egypt. First, a line of people wielded picks. They attacked thick roots and gnarled stumps, loosening clods of dirt. Then came a line of people with oversized hoes. They dragged the loosened earth into piles and shoveled it into sacks. Since we had no money for wheelbarrows, the next group heaved the heavy sacks onto their backs and hauled them down the hill to be emptied. It could hardly have been more primitive.

Still, we were making progress, even if it was painfully slow. The twenty-four-hour prayer vigil continued, with people taking turns to pray one hour during the night and a half hour during the day at the site while others worked. Lunch kept coming, though many evenings we didn't know if the budget would provide the next day's sustenance. Every penny we collected went into building materials. As we left each morning, Jaime sat in the office, puzzling how to buy lunch. The cooks waited in the kitchen for the food to be provided, a familiar routine by now. It was a daily struggle, but somehow we never went hungry, though meat became a distant memory, and sometimes lunch didn't arrive until midafternoon. We were living a prolonged miracle.

After a few days, the hard work began to hit the group. Initial enthusiasm waned. Grim silence replaced chatter and laughter as fatigue took over and the sun burned into our backs. I gave up jogging. My feet hurt all the time. I had no time or energy left and felt as though I was getting plenty of exercise anyway.

One day, two new volunteers showed up. These young men told me this was a great adventure. They ran over and grabbed a pick each, since that was the hardest work. They worked right beside me, and their conversation was entertaining to listen to, if harder to swallow than our endless cornmeal mush.

"Boy, this is great!" one enthused. He attacked a root as if it were an invading Mongol. "I love this sort of thing."

"Yeah," said the other. "For every blow of my pick, a soul comes into the Kingdom!"

I was working at a pace designed to get as much done as possible while still leaving me alive and breathing at six o'clock. These two had no such mundane concerns. They worked at an impossible rate under the torrid sun. By noon their conversation had stopped. Their hands bled where blisters had broken. Their work crawled to a near-stop. That evening they came up to me as I limped over to put my tools into the shed.

"Jim," said one, "we believe God has called us to another ministry." The next morning they were gone.

After four weeks, we had cleared enough space to lay the first foundation. Unfortunately, I had agreed months before to speak in another part of the country, long before we made the decision to buy this land. I hated to leave for a week, but there was no other way. I left Gerson in charge of digging the foundation for the 30-by-100-foot building. Upon returning, I walked over to the site early in the morning, anxious to see the foundation.

My heart sank as I stared into a trench…two feet wide and six feet deep, running around the perimeter of what was supposed to be our first building. Oh, no! It should have been maybe a foot wide and fifteen inches deep. This was a disaster! It would take an impossible amount of concrete to fill. Of course I hadn't told them specifically how deep or wide a foundation should be. How could I have overlooked such an important detail? There was nothing to do but refill it and abandon the site. It would take time for the earth to settle enough to use this place. We were less than two months from moving day and had made virtually no progress.

We found another spot on the property where we could put up a simple structure, and we started over. But this site wouldn't allow for the larger building. Instead, a smaller one would serve as a dormitory for the singles. Then I went to each of the married men and broke the news: Each married couple would have to build their own place elsewhere on the property.

Slowly, site by site, we dug and poured foundations for each house. Larry Darby gave us a form for making homemade cement blocks. We filled it with a moist concrete mix, then pounded it on the ground to pack the mortar down into the mold. Then we carefully lifted the form off. If we were lucky, we got a block. Otherwise, it fell to pieces, and we had to start all over again.

Using our homemade blocks, we built our houses. None of us knew how to use a plumb line or trowel, but we asked around until we thought we understood the basics. Anyway, we had desperation on our side. I often took a couple of minutes to set one block.

One morning Marcelo came to where I was working.

"Jim, Rosane and I have decided to leave." He paused while I took this in. "We believe God has called us out of YWAM into some other ministry. We don't know what, just yet."

He was silent. "Well, of course you know Pam and I...all of us...want what's best for you and your family," I said. "But we also hate to lose you, Marcelo." I knew they had been going through enormous struggles, particularly financial ones. There were also the three babies to take care of, an exhausting job for anyone. They were really worn out, and maybe leaving was what they needed to do. Was the Scripture about not inheriting the land God's way of preparing us?

Marcelo shook hands with me, and I went back to work, my heart heavy. How could I lose Marcelo? He was the first Brazilian God had called to work with us. How could I continue without him beside me?

Many of our people had come because of him. He had launched so many of our effective outreaches, like Ouro Prêto. It was as if the very foundations of YWAM Brazil were being shaken apart.

I worked on in the sun, laying my cement blocks and worrying. Marcelo wasn't the only one leaving. It had only been seven weeks since we began construction, yet as our moving date approached, the flow of people leaving had become a hemorrhage. I laid another block, smoothing the mortar with my trowel. Not one of those leaving admitted the situation was too hard. Rather, each had a spiritual explanation. I sighed.

When I started working on my wall, I stretched a nylon fishing line tightly from one side to the other. I knew I was supposed to keep it tight and line up the bricks with it to keep the wall straight. But my mind wasn't on my work that day. Besides everything else, the pain in my feet was growing by the minute. I didn't notice when my line worked loose. Late that afternoon, I stepped back to look at my wall. Oh no! It was all crooked!

This was just too much. In a fit of anger, I kicked it all down, hurting my feet and making myself even more angry. Then I sat in the chill of late afternoon and brooded. Time was running out. People were bailing out, including key leaders. The simplest jobs were almost impossible—we didn't know what we were doing, and we didn't have the money for proper tools. And my feet were killing me. Just as I gave a particularly deep sigh, Gerson stopped by.

"What's wrong, Jim?"

"I don't know. It just seems so impossible. I don't see how we can get done on time, and everyone is abandoning us. Marcelo told me this morning he's leaving."

Gerson sat down beside me in the rubble. "I'm not going anywhere. We'll make this thing work somehow." A rush of relief and hope swept through me. He had always indicated that he would soon move on to a Spanish-speaking country. Now his solidarity meant so much. Gerson had become my most faithful friend. As he went back to work, I started picking up the pieces of my broken wall.

"God, thank You for Gerson," I whispered. "And help us get through this, Lord. Somehow."

Before the end of the day, a couple of others told me they were going to keep fighting. I thought perhaps Gerson had told them to come by, but it still gave me courage. We would keep going.

These encouragements were very important, but my main sustenance during those difficult days came from the Lord. When I got up early and was alone with Him, I could feel His grace build back up inside me.

Several friends came by during June, walked around the property, and shook their heads. In spite of our efforts, we had accomplished so little. The opinion was unanimous: We would never make our July 12 deadline. I began to think they might be right. To complicate matters, I was committed to be on the road the first two weeks of July, speaking in churches. I had accepted the invitations a long time ago and believed strongly that once I had given my word to speak, I shouldn't break it. But how could I leave my team at such a time? We were working against the clock. July would be the coldest month, and we had to have the roofs on by the time the temperatures dipped.

SEVENTEEN

Until Dreams Come True

C O U L D you use some guys from our Bible school to help out the next ten days?" Larry Darby's question was the answer to prayer. Could we ever! And the best part was, these men actually knew how to do construction. Also, Larry went down and bought us eight wheelbarrows.

While I was off on my speaking circuit, I called back often to check on the team's progress. I was amazed when Pam said we could move on time, even though I wouldn't be there to help. As soon as possible, I headed home. I traveled on a bus all day and into the night, arriving in Belo Horizonte two hours before dawn. Most of the local buses weren't running yet, but I found one that could take me to within four miles of our property. Then I got out into the frosty darkness and walked, switching my suitcase from hand to hand.

At last, just as the sun was coming up, I came to the crest of the hill. It was the same spot where Décio had gestured vaguely in the direction of our future home. I put my suitcase down and peered at the wooded valley and hillside. It didn't look much different from when Décio first brought us out here: Just a little space cleared here and there and a few small, crude houses. I couldn't see the singles dormitory from here. It was hidden in the dusty brush.

This was home. I picked up my luggage and hurried on. At least we wouldn't be wasting money on rent. From now on our money and hard work would build something good and permanent. A cold wind blew across the land as I made my way up the hill to the two finished rooms of our house. The walls, made with our homemade blocks, hadn't been plastered yet. Everything looked raw and gray. I walked in and there was Pam in the semidarkness, stirring up a dust storm with her broom.

"Hi, Pammie, I'm home." I brushed against the wall and a small avalanche of sand fell to the floor. Pam gave me that smile I loved, with the corners turned down.

"Hi," she said. "How do you like our home?" She ran over and hugged me. It was hard to see in the room, but I looked around and saw our familiar furnishings in place. We didn't have electricity, and even the sunlight was blocked by cardboard in the window where glass would be someday.

I stood there, holding her tight. God was so good to give me Pam. Here she was in a crude little room on land carved out of the tropical bush in Brazil, but she didn't complain. Vanya toddled over and hugged my knees, then we went over together to peer into Johnnie's crib. It was so good to be back.

As soon as it warmed up a bit, I went out to look everything over. I scrambled over broken ground to the various clearings. Our water system was a well with a bucket and a rope. We had outhouses and shower stalls, where you had to carry in a bucket of water from the well to splash over yourself. There was no glass in any of our windows yet, and in most doorways we hung pieces of cloth. Almost all the floors were of beaten earth. I walked by small piles of scrap lumber covered with frost. We'd heard this was the coldest July in Belo Horizonte since 1919.

I passed a couple of the hardier souls, already at work in the early morning chill. In the past three months we had gone from ninety-six adults to thirty-two. We were totally unimpressive and very poor, but we had prevailed. We had moved onto the property. If we could only finish our buildings and pay for this land, it would be a sending center for Brazilian missionaries for years to come!

I held on to that dream as we plunged into some of the most difficult days we'd ever seen. We had no money at all, and if any did come in, we had to use it on construction. It took more than two hours to catch the two buses necessary to get downtown.

The level of evangelistic ministry dropped because of the endless man-hours we had to invest in construction. Then Vanya, who was two and a half, got sick. We found she had hepatitis. She recovered faster than expected, but still I worried. I had to provide a better place for my family and for our workers. One day I was talking to a local engineer after a meeting at the Presbyterian church. The fact that we had no electricity came up. He told me to drop by his house, and he would give me the money to get power onto the property. When I went the next week, he invited me to sit down while he wrote out a check.

"You know, Jim, not all people are called to be missionaries," he said, reaching for his checkbook. I nodded in agreement, wondering what he was getting at. "Not all nations have that calling, either. The United States is called to reach the world. Some European countries are, too."

I was silent. Now I knew where he was headed, but it didn't seem right to argue with him.

"Brazil isn't called to be a missionary country. Your effort is commendable, but Brazilians are called to win our own people." He finished writing the check and handed it to me. I thanked him for his generosity and left. If our supporters felt like this, what did others say about us?

We put in the electricity, but it was very weak, coming half a mile from the small transformer at a neighbor's farmhouse. In the evening we had to unplug all our appliances, and even then the light bulb in our room was so dim it looked like a tomato hanging from an electric wire. At peak hours there wasn't enough power to generate a television picture, but it was sure nice to have refrigeration again—at least for most of the day—and lights for night classes.

ᏋᏋ ᏋᏋ ᏋᏋ ᏋᏋ

Then a personal struggle hit hard and close. I had agreed to speak at Larry Darby's Bible school, and I took the whole family with me for the week. I always enjoyed speaking there, helping train future pastors for Brazil. But on this visit, I didn't seem to have any energy. I was speaking six hours a day, and it was sapping all my strength. After lunch I would lie down and sleep, feeling somewhat guilty. Pam was dragging herself around, too, and it suddenly was an enormous effort to keep up with our two little ones.

As soon as we got back to Belo, we went to the doctor. The diagnosis shouldn't have surprised us. We both had hepatitis. We were ordered to bed. It wasn't very restful, what with Vanya being only two years old and Jonathan still a small baby. The bathroom was an outhouse about fifty feet from our door. Baths had to be taken in the shower stall out of a bucket. We did the best we could. I didn't feel too bad, and, after three or four days, got up.

However, Pam didn't improve. She was very ill. She lay in bed and shook and moaned. Her fever soared, and the whole bed was wet with her sweat. I was scared. She shouldn't have such a fever with hepatitis. A doctor came to see her—a Peruvian with a heavy Spanish accent. While I hovered in the background, he examined Pam in our dark room. I hoped for the best, but the doctor's face was grave.

"We'll have to do some lab exams, but I believe she has strep throat along with the hepatitis." He carefully replaced the instruments in his case one by one. "You should know, sir, that the antibiotics necessary to treat the strep throat will be very hard on her while she has hepatitis." He shook his head. "We'll have to wait and see how things go."

My heart fell. Pam was so sick, yet the doctor was saying that the treatment would be too dangerous. I kept hoping and praying, but during the next two days, she got even worse, and we called the doctor again. He decided we had to fight the strep infection and injected her with a massive dose of penicillin. She looked terrible. What if I lost her?

I found a solitary spot on a hill behind our house, under a tree. I began to pace back and forth, pouring out my heart to God. "Lord, please, please heal Pam! If anything happens to her…" I choked up. The thought of life without Pam swept over me like a black void. "God, please heal her."

I hurried back to our room. It was almost time for Jonathan to wake up. He was still nursing, since Pam refused to give that up. I reached down and picked up our chubby son, laying him beside Pam. She had to nurse him lying flat on her back, since she lacked the strength to sit up. The sight of the two of them filled me with sadness and guilt. After all, I had brought them here.

"Please, Lord, spare Pam's life!" I whispered.

In a few days the penicillin took hold and Pam's temperature dropped. The crisis passed, and I breathed a sigh of relief. "Thank You, Lord!" I prayed again and again.

As the days went by, we knew Pam was getting better, even though she was still a deep shade of yellow from the hepatitis. It would be a long convalescence.

I needed to visit the team in Pôrto Alegre because they had been going through difficulties. I hated to leave Pam, but I knew our friends on the team would keep an eye on her. I was still battling hepatitis myself, though I was past the contagious stage. I got on the bus for the thirty-five-hour trip.

I stayed for a few days and did my best to encourage the team. It was especially good to see Rui and Marilac again, as well as Graça, who had come down to help them. Despite their problems, they had been leading a lot of people to Jesus. But it was Rui's story about their next-door neighbors that caught my attention.

"Jim, I've been getting up at 4:30 every morning to seek the Lord," he said. He pointed to a tent set up in the backyard where he prayed. "A lot of times, Graça joins me. Also, whenever I get a spare moment throughout the day, I go out there and pray."

He pointed to a building behind their backyard, facing the next street. "That's a spiritist center. I didn't know, but some of the times I was praying in the tent they were conducting their meetings. I guess I prayed pretty loud," he said, grinning. "Anyway, one day they came over and asked if I could refrain from praying during their meetings. They were having trouble getting their 'guides'—the possessing spirits—to come into them while we were praying!"

I remembered the young guy in the tight red pants and big Afro who had been so agitated the first time he went to church. God had done so much in Rui's life. I went back on the bus, encouraged.

We sent Paulo Sergio down to lead the work in Pôrto Alegre. He had shown the highest standards of integrity and leadership, and I knew he would handle the ministry well down there. As long as we were producing people like Paulo, Rui, and Graça, we would prevail.

I remembered how God had brought us to care for the Brazilian people. When we first saw the Amazon region from the air, we hadn't thought about the people living in that jungle. But now we really wanted to do something to help them. And when we were walking with George Foster and saw the pitiful state of the street children, we had no idea how involved we would be in helping meet their needs. We wanted to do so much. And there was our big dream: Someday, we'd see Brazilians going all over the world.

Sometimes, though, usually late at night, I wondered if we could survive until our dreams came true.

EIGHTEEN

Seeing Clearly

GERSON led the second New Year's Eve outreach during the spiritist gathering in Rio. We had gotten bolder and decided to recruit young people from local churches. Sixty participated and reported having a really good time. We prayed that someday hundreds of Christians would come to the beaches and take authority over the darkness.

However, Gerson had more distant horizons on his mind. He took a small team up to the northeast where the Catholics put on an elaborate passion play every year. Thousands came to drink and party during the festival, so it was a great place to evangelize.

I went north and joined Gerson, Elisa, and the team. We prayed with many to give their lives to Jesus. Also, in between the street meetings and going out to talk to people, I had some time with Gerson. He wanted to start another center here in the north, and he and his team were praying about what to do next.

One day, just before I was due to leave on a bus for Belo, I found Gerson in the back of the place where we'd been staying, butchering a goat for the midday meal. "Hello, Jim," Gerson said, hunched over a water spigot, cutting up the meat into a tin basin. "It sure is a shame you won't be at lunch! This is going to make a very fine barbecue." He laughed.

"Yeah, Gerson, I know you're really broken up!" I sat on the grass and watched as he expertly carved the meat into little strips and flicked them into a basin.

"We've finally made up our minds," he said. "Elisa and I believe God is calling us to minister in the Amazon. We want to start in Belém."

I knew Belém, a city near the Atlantic Ocean in the delta region of the Amazon river system. "That's great, Gerson. We'll sure miss you in Belo. But it'll be tremendous to see YWAM get started in the Amazon."

As I rode home on the bus, I thought of how much I would miss Gerson. How I would love to be up there with his team! At last we were going to have a part in reaching the Stone-Age tribes hidden in those vast jungles. Back home, I began to feel very weary. It had been four years of constant struggle. I had asked God several times why we had such severe problems. I asked Him this when I thought we were going to lose our first child, and again when I was praying in the black hole under the stairs. He hadn't answered me yet.

I took up jogging again. One afternoon I was on my daily run, and things weren't going well. I felt as though I had sand in my joints and my lungs had dried into old leather. Every part of my body seemed heavier than it should have been. My muscles jerked and jarred me along, refusing to develop any smooth rhythm as I ran. And to make matters worse, it had rained earlier in the afternoon, and now the sun had come out again. It was like slogging through a sauna as wisps of steam rose from the damp, red earth around me.

I started to pray as I ran, more to take my mind off my misery than out of any particular spiritual expectation. "Father, I love You and thank You for the privilege of serving You. You are perfect in all

Your ways. Thank You for being with me. Can we talk and take my mind off this run?"

Jim, why are you running? He spoke into my mind.

I was puzzled. Surely God didn't need a lecture on cardiovascular fitness. But I answered, "Well, Lord, it's good for my body."

Does your body like it?

"Are You kidding? Today it thinks I'm trying to kill it."

Do you hate your body?

"No. I'm running because I care about it."

Would your body prefer to be somewhere else, and doing something else?

"Sure. If I left it up to my body, I would be stretched out in front of a fan with an ice-cold Coke and nachos with guacamole!"

Why don't you do your body a favor and do that?

"It wouldn't be a favor. It would just be easier and more comfortable."

Do you mean easy and comfortable aren't always the best?

Revelation started to penetrate. I thought about the Bible verse that says all things work together for good. "Good" doesn't necessarily mean "easy" or "comfortable." And the very next verse talks about being conformed to the image of Christ.

As I jogged through the tropical sunset, I saw more clearly. God had never forgotten us or been harsh with us. He didn't love us less than those who seemed to have it so easy. We had given Him our lives. We had pledged to be faithful whatever the cost. We had asked Him to transform us. He was taking us at our word and carefully molding us.

"Father, I see," I said. "Please forgive me...I've complained so much...I've been full of unbelief. This must have hurt You. I'm sorry." I forced my tired body to take me over the crest of the last hill. I was almost back to our property.

"Lord, I embrace the difficulties You've put in our lives. Please don't give up on us, Lord. Keep us stretching toward Your ideals for us."

I arrived back at our gray, unfinished house, panting and dripping with sweat, but newly determined. We'd been on the property ten months now, but I sensed that something new and important was about to happen. God was preparing me for something.

That night I went to teach the evening class for our current group of thirty students. I felt fine when I went in, but halfway through my teaching session something strange started to happen in my body. My right side turned numb. I could still move my right arm and leg—I just couldn't feel them. I didn't say anything about how I felt but kept trying to teach. Several times I stumbled over sentences, losing the flow of my thoughts. Finally, my lecture was over, and I went to find the nurse we had on staff. What if they discovered me unconscious during the night? The only thing I thought it could be was the beginning of a stroke. I told the nurse my symptoms. She took my pulse and looked closely into my eyes.

"I don't see any outward signs. Sorry, but I don't have the instruments to take your blood pressure. Your pulse seems normal. Get some rest and see a doctor first thing tomorrow."

Pam was already asleep, so I slipped in beside her and tried to put the fear out of my mind. I woke with a terrible pain in my head. It was still dark in the room, so I reached for a flashlight. It was only midnight. I tried to sleep, but the pain was too intense, blocking out every other thought. Later in the night I got irritated…someone was moaning, and it was bothering me.

The next day as the pain started subsiding, I realized the groans had come from me! I went to the doctor, and he did all sorts of tests. He never told me what had happened but prescribed some pills and a lot of rest, and forbade travel.

During the next two weeks I had three more mysterious attacks. Each time I would be totally unaware of my surroundings. Even when I wasn't in pain, parts of my right side would tingle and go numb. What if I had to cut back on my activities? What if I couldn't physically continue in my calling?

NINETEEN

"If God Were in This…"

A TELEGRAM arrived on Monday announcing a gift and presenting a challenge. A Brazilian girl was in training at YWAM's university in Hawaii, one of four or five students who had managed to break through our national boundaries to train overseas. She sent a telegram saying that a married couple had offered her $1,000 for expenses to attend a YWAM international leadership conference in Thailand. It started in four days, on Thursday. She believed God had told her to give me the money so I could go.

I showed Pam the telegram. "What do you think?" she asked. "Have you prayed about whether or not you should go?"

We had gotten the conference invitation months before, but I had ignored it. "It's not like we have trouble deciding what to do with our money around here," I countered.

I didn't want to admit to Pam that, no, it hadn't crossed my mind to ask the Lord if I should go. People living on cornmeal mush and taking cold showers out of a bucket don't go running off around the world, do they? Besides, my body seemed to be falling apart.

Pam didn't say anything, but I knew what she was thinking. We weren't supposed to be guided by whether we had the money or not. At least, that's what I taught our students about faith and finances.

The first step was to call the girl for more information. We had no telephone, so it took me most of the next day, Tuesday, to get into town, place an overseas call, and reach the Brazilian student in Hawaii. Yes, she said, she did believe I should go instead of her. She didn't actually have the money yet. It was still in Australian dollars rather than American. I said I'd let her know what I decided.

The conference started in less than three days. If I were to go I would have to leave by the next night—Wednesday—and even then, I'd be a little late. This wasn't like jumping on a plane in the States, either. Like any Brazilian citizen or resident, I'd have to go through a whole bureaucratic process to get permission from the government to leave. It was already too late to get all that done. It was impossible.

Still, if God were in this....

I decided to go to town first thing in the morning. Our blue van had suffered a major accident and died, leaving us without transportation again. It would take me more than two hours to get downtown by walking two miles, then catching two different buses. If I were to stay home to pray about it in the morning and the Lord said to go, I wouldn't have time to act on His instructions. I'd have to get downtown first, then pray.

I set off very early Wednesday with my Bible clutched in my hand and confusion swirling in my mind. I had time to think as I walked down the dusty road, then waited forty minutes for the first bus. I didn't have any money. The promised offering wouldn't get me all the way to Thailand, let alone back home. And if I had one of those attacks in an airplane, I could be in big trouble. My last attack had been less than a week before, and as I thought about it, I could feel the tingling in my right shoulder, hip, and the side of my head.

Besides, how could I justify a trip to Thailand when we didn't know where our next meal was coming from? On the other hand, why had the money been offered? Was it from God? Would I miss something important if I didn't go? The more I thought about it the more confused I got.

Finally I reached the center of the city, sat on a bench in the praça, and looked around. Hundreds of people rushed by as Belo Horizonte started another business day. Hawkers shouted their wares. Street kids woke and crawled out from under cardboard boxes. A blind man sold lottery tickets, and a natural healer with a snake coiled around his arm expounded the benefits of his elixir. This wasn't much of a prayer closet, but it would have to do.

"Lord," I prayed, "what should I do? This all seems crazy. I should have asked You weeks ago whether to go or not. Yet, it doesn't seem humanly possible to go. But then again, doing possible things hasn't seemed to be the way You have led us before! Should I go, Lord? I submit to Your will, but I don't know what it is. Please speak to me, Father."

Car horns blared and several buses passed the praça, belching black clouds of pollution. Then God spoke in my mind. He gave me three Scripture references to look up. They were in different books of the Bible, but each one spoke of the twelve spies whom Moses had sent to spy out the land. Ten were rejected because they didn't believe God despite impossible circumstances. Caleb and Joshua were the exceptions. They followed the Lord fully. I understood. There was something about this trip that was very important to God, and He wanted me to go. I still didn't want to, but that was irrelevant. I wanted to follow the Lord fully, like Joshua and Caleb.

I got up from the bench and hurried to the travel agency where a Brazilian friend named Brás worked. He had helped us before, handling the bureaucratic red tape that consumed weeks of time. How on earth could I persuade him to try to do the impossible and get my documentation by that night?

I found him seated at his desk in a large office he shared with five others.

"Brás, I need to leave on a trip tonight. I'll need the necessary permission from the government by this afternoon."

"That's impossible! It takes several days. The quickest I've ever seen it happen was in twenty-four hours."

"I need it by this afternoon. I have to catch a flight to Rio."

"But it can't be done."

"It's okay," I said. "I know you can't guarantee it. Just do your best. Whatever happens is fine." I felt at peace. This was God's responsibility. Going to Thailand was His idea, not mine.

From there I went to a pay phone and called a friend at Betânia, asking if I could use his credit card until the offering arrived from Hawaii. He assured me that would be fine; I could use his Varig card, as long as I traveled with that airline and repaid him in thirty days. With that step taken care of, I crossed the avenue and pushed back the glass doors into the air-conditioned comfort of the Varig offices. A Brazilian girl, sophisticated and efficient-looking in her uniform, looked up from her paperwork.

"How far can I get toward Asia with a thousand Australian dollars?" I smiled as her official expression dropped and she fixed me with an intensely curious stare. It was an odd question. She checked her prices in a thick book. "You could get as far as Honolulu, Hawaii, sir."

"Fine. I'll take a ticket for tonight."

She clicked away on the computer for a few moments and then explained. "I'm sorry, sir. I can get you on the last flight to Rio, but we have no places open on tonight's flight out of there. We can get you a reservation for two weeks from now."

"Sorry, it's tonight or nothing. Could you keep trying?"

"I can, but I can't give you any hope of success. There isn't even room to put you on the waiting list."

"That's all right," I said, smiling. "I understand. I'll be in this afternoon to pick up my ticket."

She opened her mouth as if to say something, then snapped it closed. I grinned and decided not to explain anything. Better to be considered a man of mystery than a semi-insane religious fanatic!

I rushed to the bus stop to head back to the base. It was 11 a.m. I had only five hours to get home on two buses, walk a mile and a half, pack, say goodbye, and get back to catch my plane for Rio, then on to Los Angeles and Hawaii.

When I told Pam I was going to Thailand on a one-way ticket that would only get me as far as Hawaii, she didn't even blink. She helped me pack my suitcase, found a sitter for the kids, and headed back to town with me to see me off. I went first to Brás. As I walked into his office he was shaking his head, half excited and half unbelieving.

"I don't understand," he said. "This just doesn't happen. Your papers are ready. The messenger is on his way right now."

We sat in Brás' office and waited. Half an hour went by. Now it was only an hour until my flight left for Rio. Finally, the messenger walked in, and we grabbed my travel documents, heading out the door to the airline office.

It was 6 p.m. when we walked into Varig, and almost everyone was gone. Then I saw the girl who had waited on me that morning. She smiled and shook her head, just as Brás had done. "I don't get it," she said. "I checked ten minutes ago just so I could tell you I had, and the computer accepted your name for a reservation on tonight's flight. I don't know how that happened."

I smiled in what I hoped was an enigmatic way and waited. She finished filling out my ticket and handed it to me. "I'm sorry for the delay. Although you have a ticket, you don't have time now to catch the flight from Belo to Rio. The plane leaves in thirty minutes."

"It will be all right."

I was totally unconcerned. If God wanted me to go, He would make a way. If not, I'd rather stay home anyway.

Pam and I went outside and caught a cab. It was twenty minutes until my flight was scheduled to take off for Rio. Our cab wove through traffic, taking thirty minutes to get to the airport. We walked in to learn that the flight had been delayed. I had just enough time to check in, kiss Pam goodbye, and fly to Rio.

TWENTY

Sharing the Vision

T H E ticket agent frowned as she typed my name into the computer. I couldn't quite see the monitor, no matter how hard I craned my neck. "What is it? Isn't my reservation in the computer?" I asked.

"It's worse than that. Could you wait over there until I call you, sir?"

"Sure, no problem," I said with a smile.

I stood by a column and watched. She called a whole bevy of supervisors and officials over. What was going on? They were consulting with one another and frantically poking at the keyboard, stealing an occasional glance in my direction. I wondered if one or two of them might be from the federal police. Had I gotten my visa so rapidly because it didn't go through the proper channels? Would they turn me back now?

"Lord," I prayed quietly, "I'm at peace. Whatever it is, I put it in Your hands. I'm not going to fight to go on this flight. I'd actually rather go back home. If You want me to go, You'd better do something now. It's up to You." Suddenly everyone at the check-in counter smiled and started chattering, looking relieved. They dispersed, and the woman called me over to check in for the flight to Los Angeles.

I never discovered the reason for the fuss. I got on the plane with a one-way ticket that wouldn't get me where I was going and wouldn't get me back home again, either. This was definitely not what the doctor had in mind when he told me to avoid travel and take it easy. Would I get sick and stranded, or would God's name be glorified somehow? I put my head back against the airline pillow and tried to sleep. My right hip and shoulder were tingling ominously.

When I arrived in L.A. I called ahead and told my father-in-law I was coming to Honolulu on my way to Thailand. I also called Loren Cunningham's office and said I was on my way to Thailand but would be at my in-laws' until I got the rest of the money. They understood, since others in YWAM did crazy things like this. But what would I tell my father-in-law?

He met my plane, looking as dignified as ever. We greeted each other and were soon headed out on Pali Highway through the green mountain passes toward their house.

"So, Jim, you're going to Thailand?" he asked politely, smoothly changing into a faster lane of traffic.

"That's right. Our mission is having an international leadership conference there."

"Did you see on the news that the Vietnamese are bombing in Thailand somewhere?"

"No, I haven't seen any newspapers."

"It sounds dangerous. Do you still think you should go?"

"Yes, I think so."

"Well, when do you leave?"

This was getting uncomfortable. I wanted Pam's dad to think highly of me. How could I tell him I didn't have a ticket to continue my trip? I tried to be as vague as possible. "I have to go soon. The conference starts tomorrow."

"No, what I want to know is, when is your flight? We have to know when to get you back to the airport." There was no escape. I could only tell the truth. "I don't have an onward ticket. I believe God wants me to go, and I will wait for Him to provide a ticket. So I don't know the details of my flight yet."

He looked at me as if I were a newly discovered and quite amazing life form. Then he took a firmer grip on the steering wheel and showed a whole new concentration on his driving. We came out of the Pali tunnel and headed into the green valley of the windward side of Oahu. At least there were no more embarrassing questions. There was no more conversation at all.

I stayed with Pam's folks for two days. I knew the conference had already begun, but there was nothing I could do. My father-in-law told his wife that I had no ticket, and she came to me like a co-conspirator. She thought her auto mechanic might help, since he was an outspoken Christian. She introduced me to the mechanic, and he gave me $200. I appreciated it, but I needed about $2,000 to complete my trip. Then I got a telephone call from Loren's office.

"Loren asked me to call you," Loren's assistant said. "The other leaders at the conference heard about your situation and want you to come. Some of the European leaders want to lend money for your ticket...but they want to know if you could go home by way of Europe. They would like to book you for some speaking engagements. They would take up offerings and you could pay them back for the ticket."

It didn't take me a minute to say, yes, I'd love to go by Europe on my way home! Maybe that was why God went to all that trouble to get me out of Brazil, so that more people would know what was happening in Brazil.

My mother-in-law was disappointed, though. She wanted to see a really dramatic miracle. I hugged them both and got on the plane for Thailand for what turned out to be a historic leadership conference for our mission. Among other important decisions, YWAM agreed to launch ministries to help the poor and needy in a big way. I smiled to myself. What we had already done—taking in orphans—was now official.

Also, I was introduced during the course of the meetings. I was surprised how many of the leaders didn't know YWAM was working in Brazil. On my way home I ministered in Germany, Greece, Switzerland, Holland, and England. At each stop I asked if anyone knew YWAM was active in Brazil. Generally, no one did. Maybe this trip would start linking us more strongly with YWAM in the rest of the world. I was beginning to understand why God had so dramatically led me on this trip.

The YWAMers gave generously in Europe. I headed home thirty days after I left, with enough money to pay for my travel plus buy our own transformer. Now we could leave our refrigerators plugged in at night! The money from the girl in Hawaii didn't come in for weeks, after I had already paid everything.

Pam met me at the Belo airport with a big hug. She had brought along Vanya and Johnnie, and soon my arms were full. It was great to be back! As we made our way home on the bus, Pam asked, "So how did you do physically? Have you had any more of those attacks?" Then I realized that I had experienced no numbness or pain. Nothing. Not since that little bit of tingling when I left Rio.

Seeing our modest community after a month away filled me with gratitude. It might take time to make the transition from hotels, airports, and European YWAM centers back to our rugged base in Belo Horizonte. Yet in spite of the grimness of our situation, I had a strong feeling of homecoming, not only to my family, but also to Brazil and to Belo. This was where God was working out His purposes in our lives. I could hardly wait to see what came next.

TWENTY-ONE

A Door to the Amazon

EARLY one morning about nine months after my return from Thailand, Pam hurried into our house carrying something wrapped in a dirty blanket. "Look, Jim, it's a baby. Doesn't it just break your heart?"

I peered into the bundle and saw a tiny black face covered with scabs and running sores. "Good grief! He's in terrible shape! Whose is he?"

"*He* is a she," Pam corrected me. "And we're not positive where she came from. This morning Noecir found her on the steps of his church. Someone must have left her there during the night. Poor thing."

We had twenty-two in our orphanage now—with no room for even one more. We took the baby to the doctor and found out she was five months old, although she weighed only half of what a normal child that age should. She was suffering from severe malnutrition and a terrible skin infection. Pam decided she would nurse the baby to health, and we kept her in our home. This was no easy task. The baby cried constantly from the pain of her infection. I felt guilty about leaving Pam every day with this new burden. She even had to boil the baby's clothes, sheets, and towels to control the skin condition.

A local pastor knew who the baby's parents were. Like so many in Brazil, they had trouble feeding all their children. Out of five, only she and a brother were still alive, and that brother was blind from prolonged malnutrition.

Gradually, the baby got better, and when she stopped crying all the time, she was a cute little thing. She was able to sit on my lap now and curl her tiny black finger around my fat white one. I started to dread giving her up. One evening, just after putting the three little ones to bed, Pam curled up next to me on the couch where I was reading. By now we had plastered and painted the inside of our bedrooms, and even had added a bathroom with running water. With the help of some used furniture and the turquoise and black trimmed rug our Betânia friends had given us long ago, it was looking pretty homey.

"Jim, I've been wondering…." She paused, and I laid down my book. "I think we ought to keep this little baby."

I knew she had gotten really attached in the two months she had nursed the tot back to health. But keep her? "I'm not sure her parents will let us adopt her, Pam. It could be quite a hassle getting them to agree."

"I know, but I think it's something we should try to do."

I agreed to pray about it. I soon knew this little girl was to be part of our family. We couldn't take in every unwanted child in Brazil…there were millions. But we could take those God gave us, just as if they were born to us.

It was an enormous effort to persuade her parents, then go through all the red tape, but finally she was ours. We named her Maile, like the fragrant leaves they use to make leis in Hawaii.

❧ ❧ ❧ ❧

Gerson and Elisa and their team had been in Belém for six months now, and I traveled forty-eight hours by bus to join their outreach during a religious festival. It was great to see Gerson and the others. They were living in the dock area, in a wooden house built on stilts over the Guamá River. I stood looking across this one part of the Amazon basin and felt overwhelmed. It was huge. The other side was just a low green line on the distant horizon. I watched as barges, launches, and tiny canoes plied the muddy waters, and thought about where they were going, where they'd been, and of the Indians in the vast jungles beyond. The air was alive with adventure.

Belém's streets were already filling with people. One million came from all over the Amazon for this festival called "Círio de Nazaré." Gerson's team and I crowded onto the buses crammed with natives. Some showed strong native Indian features, others had Latin faces, while others revealed African parentage. Thirty of us YWAMers were here for the festival to share our faith with these people.

On the first night, Gerson and I decided to go to the Catholic church for the highlight of the festival—when they took the image of Mary in a procession through the streets of Belém. We struggled for blocks through the seething mass of people pressing their way to the church. Finally we could see the gleaming white cathedral, outlined with thousands of tiny white lights.

It was extremely uncomfortable with so many people jammed together in the hot, humid street. Finally the great moment arrived, a band struck up a tune, and ten important-looking men came out the front doors. There were four priests in elaborate robes, accompanied by men in suits, probably local authorities. Following closely on their heels was an exquisitely canopied platform with long poles resting on the shoulders of eight men. Under the canopy was a small statue of Mary, dressed in a gown that looked like woven gold.

Tens of thousands of firecrackers were set off at once, and a haze hung over the street. Everyone went crazy, clapping and cheering and clawing their way toward the image. I thought we were about to be crushed to death. Ropes on either side of the street held back the crowd, but they fought to get closer.

"They believe if they can just help carry that rope through the city, then the idol will bless them," explained Gerson. Then I noticed that everyone holding on to the rope was barefoot. Gerson said these penitents would hang on desperately as the procession wound up and down the streets, struggling to keep their hands on the rope and stay upright until their feet were cut and bleeding.

I felt saddened and angered by the whole display. I was anxious to start introducing people to the Lord who would truly meet their needs. We went to work evangelizing during the days and into the evenings, praying with several hundred people over the next fifteen days.

One warm evening, Gerson and I sat in a sidewalk café, relaxing after a busy day. There were still thousands partying in the street. Gerson took a long sip of his Coke. "Jim, I feel like God is telling us to do something up here." He watched for my reaction. I waited. "We think the Lord wants us to start working among the Amazon Indians."

"That's terrific, Gerson. Really."

"But to get started, we want to send some of our workers to Wycliffe to study linguistics. Is that a problem?"

I assured him that it was fine. It was more than fine. Wycliffe provided excellent training. And this might be our first step to reaching the Indians. Their situation was pitiful. I had heard there were at least 150 different Indian groups who had never been reached with the gospel. Many of these groups were dying out before hearing about Jesus—thousands had been killed by measles or even common colds after contact with outsiders.

Even sadder were those Indians who felt so depressed and inferior after their first contact with civilization that they would refuse to have any more babies, smother the ones that were born, or even commit group suicide by taking curare—a poisonous plant in the jungle. And there were also the cases where miners, loggers, and ranchers had hunted down Indians like animals and slaughtered them. The greed was so great and the Amazon territory so enormous that authorities couldn't always prevent or punish such things. It was a massive, ongoing tragedy.

We sat in the sidewalk café into the night as Gerson told me their plans to reach the Indians. They would start a Discipleship Training School here in Belém, and then a school to teach linguistics and jungle survival skills.

❧ ❧ ❧ ❧

The bus broke down three times, and it took me fifty-six hours traveling day and night to get back home. I spent much of the time thinking about the challenges ahead for the Belém team. They had very little committed financial support—almost none. And getting to the remote Indians would be a costly affair, traveling by large passenger riverboats, then hiring smaller ones to go up the tributaries.

When I saw Gerson and Elisa again eight months later, on their way to visit Elisa's family in Argentina, they were frustrated. Our students had done well at the Wycliffe linguistics school. Three of our girls had been the best in their class. But there was no money nor transport to get them out to the tribes. And where would the girls go first? I didn't know how to help them.

The answer came unexpectedly and dramatically, without any assistance from me. I first heard about it when Gerson and Elisa came through again a month later, on their way back from Argentina. "Jim, Pam, you won't believe this," Gerson said, grinning a little. Elisa just smiled quietly. The four of us were together in our small sitting room. "No, you could never imagine," he said.

"Well, what is it?"

He looked at Elisa with a twinkle in his eye. Then finally he said, "Oh, it's nothing much...we're just sending our first workers to an Amazon Indian tribe!"

"What happened?"

"It all started with this letter…but I'm getting ahead of myself. After we left here last month on our way to Argentina, Elisa and I visited this friend named Paulo Roberto, a pastor down south in Maringá who worked among the Amazon Indians years ago.

"Paulo showed us this letter from an Indian chief called Cadete, chief of the Atuka group of the Sateré Indians. Paulo Roberto had met him during his time in the Amazon. Cadete wanted help for his people but didn't know how to get it. This group isn't as isolated as some, but he waited more than a year before he saw another white man—a trader. Seeing his opportunity, he sat the trader down and dictated a letter for Paulo."

Gerson explained that the trader happened to be a Christian, and he tracked down Paulo Roberto's address in the south of Brazil and sent him the letter. "Here's a photocopy." Gerson unfolded a piece of paper from his pocket. I quickly read the faded words and passed it to Pam. It was a real Macedonian call. This chief was asking for someone to come tell his people the ways of God and teach their children to read and write. He promised to build a hut for whoever came and to feed him fish, meal, and fruit. He was literally begging for a missionary.

"Paulo Roberto was so sad," Gerson went on. "He explained that though he couldn't go himself, he took this letter to churches and Bible schools in two states. He sent copies to everyone he could think of. But he couldn't find anyone willing to go."

"And…," I prompted.

"So I told him, 'Paulo, we have two girls ready and waiting right now. They're trained in linguistics. They could go to the Atukas next week if they had the money. Telling Paulo that was like throwing gasoline on a fire! He asked us to speak in his church. We attended a week of services with about a hundred of his members, plus visitors. You wouldn't believe what happened at the last meeting, Jim. God touched those people, and they turned their pockets inside out. A young couple who had just finished making payments on an expensive guitar put it in the offering to be sold. Another family promised their entertainment center, and a businessman bought it on the spot, putting the money in the offering. A boy gave his bicycle. An elderly woman gave her pension check, all she had to live on that month. A young man promised his new motorcycle.

"You know what the offering was when they totaled all they got from the items sold? Eight thousand dollars! Pretty good, huh?" Gerson finished, grinning.

Gerson and Elisa headed back to Belém and bought a one-cylinder diesel boat for workers going to the Indians. We were glad for this small start and prayed that someday we could make an impact on the sad situation of the indigenous peoples of the Amazon. Now if we could just see some victories in our situation in Belo. We would not only send workers to the Amazon, but to the whole world! But it had been a year and a half since we moved, and we still hadn't paid anything on the property. I had gone to Décio and asked him to define the size of our payments and the date they should start, but he hadn't answered me on either of the questions.

I was growing more and more uneasy. It seemed like something was bothering him—something he wasn't telling me. Finally one day as I sat in his cluttered office, he told me what was wrong.

"You know, brother, our inflation is seventy percent a year now. All my brothers and sisters have to sign this contract, and they won't accept the plan you and I originally agreed upon." My heart sank as I waited for details.

"They want a good down payment." He shifted in his chair, looking as though he didn't want to share the specifics.

"How much are we talking about?"

"I think the minimum down payment they want is $7,500, to be paid in a month or two. You can get that from your American supporters, can't you?"

Yeah, right, I thought. Our American support still added up to a grand total of $400 a month, from that one church in Hawaii. The rest came in somehow, always a miracle and always unexpected. But I tried to sound confident.

"We'll trust God that the money will be there." My stomach felt like lead, but Décio had been so good to us, I wasn't going to burden him with my problems.

TWENTY-TWO

Breaking Through with Prayer

I WENT back to the base and called a time of fasting and prayer for the next day. Only God could help us. The amount was huge—$7,500 was what twelve Brazilian laborers would make in a whole year.

Twenty of our staff gathered early in the morning to seek the Lord. We were sitting on backless wooden benches in a little room with a dirt floor and no window glass. I reviewed the situation to everyone; then we began to pray. It was hard, heavy going. When I prayed, it was like talking to the walls and the ceiling. Others took turns praying. The pauses between prayers got longer and longer. I checked my watch. We'd only been going an hour. I closed my eyes.

Oh, God, help us, I prayed silently. *We can't even pray!* I got down on my knees and pressed my head down on the cold bench. Someone prayed something about our trust being in the Lord, and how she knew He'd come through. The hours crept by.

The lunch hour came and went, but we weren't eating, of course. About 2 p.m., something happened. A new energy came into our prayers. Everyone started praying at once, very loudly. Many lifted their hands, their eyes closed, tears running down their faces. After a few minutes, we were quiet again, but with a different kind of quietness.

"I believe it's done," one of our guys said.

"I agree; God just spoke to me and said the victory is ours," said a young woman.

Someone started singing a chorus of praise, and we all joined in at the top of our voices, worshiping the Lord. We knew He had heard us. God had said it was going to happen. We stayed there late into the afternoon and shared specific ideas we had gotten during the prayer time—people to contact about the need. We even took up an offering among ourselves and came up with about $200.

Several days later I was in Rio de Janeiro speaking to a gathering of pastors. They gave us $600. A friend from the States sent $2,000. Brazilian YWAMers were blessed with gifts and turned around and gave toward the payment. Little by little it came in, and before the due date, we were able to go to Décio and pay. What a relief!

As soon as we made the down payment it was time to start paying the $600 monthly installments. How were we going to handle that? Then I caught myself...I felt deeply embarrassed for doubting the Lord. Hadn't He supplied everything we needed for years now? Hadn't He just brought in $7,500 for a down payment? How could I doubt Him? I repented of my unbelief. Then, within days, I was worrying again.

Over the next few months my fears seemed justified. With only five small houses, one dormitory, and a crude cooking house built, we had to stop construction. We had dug the foundation for a much-needed larger building with a dining room/meeting hall and more dorm space. But we couldn't go any further. The $600 monthly payments were eating up all our income.

Our ministry efforts continued to grow and encourage us. It was almost time for our next outreach at the New Year's Eve spiritist celebration in Rio. What had started somewhat timidly was now an all-out effort. I looked forward to going on the beaches and seeing God push back the paganism.

The day after Christmas, a hot summer scorcher, I left by bus for Rio. One church hosted us, but we had more than 350 volunteers from all sorts of churches participating. Quite a difference from three years before, when pastors warned their people to stay away from the spiritist event.

However, nothing I had seen on television of the Iemanjá celebration prepared me for what I saw as I walked out on Copacabana Beach that sultry evening. It was like entering the devil's fair. Competing spiritist centers had altars up and down the four-mile beach. Myriads of idols shone dully with the flicker of millions of candles. Among the images you would see an occasional Jesus, but pride of place was given to Iemanjá, the beautiful young goddess of the seas with her long black hair, white complexion, and sweeping white robes. Mary also occupied a place of honor in the eclectic blend.

I walked through the throngs where everyone was dressed in white. At the water's edge tiny lavish boats were heaped with offerings for Iemanjá. Common people gave cigars and cachaça, a sugar-cane brandy, while the wealthy worshipers gave expensive jewelry. At midnight the gift-laden boats would be pushed into the sea. If the ocean took them out, it was a good omen for the coming year. If it didn't, appeasements would be made to the spirit world.

At twilight thousands of drums began to beat along the beach. The spiritists started dancing in circles and chanting. Already some were twisting into impossible shapes and stumbling around in the sand, moaning as their "spirit guides" entered them. Around each group eager lines of petitioners formed, ready to ask the possessed person to bless them or give predictions for the new year.

I watched as young, fresh-faced teenagers crowded into the lines, as well as professional-looking middle-aged people and elderly folks. Perhaps many were here simply out of curiosity, drawn by the magnitude of the event. I turned away, sickened at the thought of a million people opening themselves up to all this darkness. I hurried back to our stage, where we had an enormous, borrowed public-address system set up. Throughout the night we would be spiritual lifeguards on the beach, saving as many as we could.

The sounds of guitars and Christian praise songs began to compete bravely with the drums and the chanting. Soon we drew several hundred to our stage, where we preached about Jesus Christ—the only one who can save us.

As soon as one sermon concluded and the invitation was given, we had counselors ready to pray with people while others started the meeting over, praising God and preaching our hearts out. We took demon-possessed people aside where special counseling teams were ready to help them.

In addition to our program on the stage, we had small prayer teams posted up and down the beach, quietly resisting the action of the enemy, especially in the lives of those drawn there out of curiosity. As the night wore on, we handed out 120,000 booklets about spiritism and the Bible.

By the time the sky above Copacabana turned pink and New Year's Day dawned, each of our 350 Christian workers had given a full witness of Christ to thirty or forty people, plus a short word to many more. We were exhausted but felt great. Life didn't get much better than this.

Several months went by. Reports came in from Gerson and the team. He and another fellow had taken two YWAM girls out to work in the village of Chief Cadete, where the letter asking for help had come from. Gerson wrote to invite me to come with him to the jungle and visit the team. Would I ever!

It took the usual forty-eight hours to get to Belém, and Gerson met my bus. The team loaned me a hammock, mosquito net, and other things I would need for our trip. We would be gone at least a month.

Travel in the Amazon is unique. We'd start on a large triple-decker catamaran the government took on regular runs along the one thousand-mile route from Belém to Manaus. We'd take the boat as far as

Parintins, get off there, and, hopefully, find a boat leaving for Maués. After we got to Maués, we'd have to hire a small boat to get us out to Atuka, the Sateré village where our girls were living and working.

Finally, the night came for us to leave Belém. When we got to the boat, hundreds of people had already claimed their places, hanging their hammocks where they wanted to spend the next five days and nights. Gerson and I avoided the wire cages where passengers were supposed to stay and established ourselves in the hallway. In each cage, hammocks hung three or four deep in a stinking, stifling crush of humanity. Within a few hours, I realized I wasn't much better off, for I had hung my hammock right in front of the smokestack, and it was very hot. Gerson had some good laughs about my situation.

Soon we were sailing smoothly over the water, and by morning, the Amazon stretched everywhere we could see. It looked more like a brown ocean instead of a river.

The six hundred people crammed on board had nothing to do for five days and nights, so Gerson and I decided to preach to them on the recreation deck. Gerson played his guitar to gather a small crowd, then we'd take turns preaching. Soon we had our hands full talking to people about Jesus.

We got off in Parintins and were fortunate to find a boat leaving immediately for Maués, where friends of Gerson fired up their small motorboat to take us out to the village. Gerson said the trip from Belém often took more than two weeks, but we made it in six days and nights.

It was already dark by the time our boat pulled into the last inlet. A large group greeted us on the riverbank. I could seek the outline of several thatched shelters and the glow of half a dozen fires on the hill above the river. We stepped out of the boat into squishy mud and were met by Márcia's and Elci's enthusiastic embraces.

"It's wonderful to have you here!" Elci cried. "Thank you so much for coming!"

The girls presented us to Chief Cadete, who didn't look at all like I expected an Amazon chief to look. He was short and trim, dressed in simple cotton shorts like the river people, but his eyes were shrewd. He greeted us with reserved dignity, and we climbed the sandy hillside together, passing through the crowd of barrel-chested, bandy-legged Indians.

Both girls started to chatter—evidently they were starved to talk to someone from home.

We went into Cadete's large hut, which like all the others in the settlement had no walls, and we squatted before his fire. I watched as Márcia managed to translate our conversation into the Sateré language. She seemed very proficient, considering how little time the girls had been there. No food was evident, but we were shown where to hang our hammocks in Cadete's hut.

The next morning, Gerson and I were anxious to get a report from Márcia and Elci. Again, there was no mention of breakfast, so we got a drink from the girls' water containers. Then Elci, Gerson, and I went paddling out to fish in one of the Indian's canoes. If we caught something, we could have lunch.

We stuck some lures in the water and paddled to troll behind us. The water in this part of the Amazon was dark, like strong tea, but amazingly clear. Gerson explained that the trees in this part of the jungle had lots of tannic acid.

As we paddled along and watched our lures, Elci filled us in on their progress. They had started a school for the village children and were having church services in the Sateré language. They were reaching out to many Sateré villages scattered throughout the region.

I handed my line to Elci and took over paddling. Only a few minutes had gone by when Elci squealed, "I have one!" She pulled in a black piranha that weighed a good three pounds. We would have lunch.

Before we went to shore, Gerson asked, "Are you thirsty?"

I sure was. By now, the sun was directly overhead, and I was very hot. "Follow me," Gerson said and jumped off the canoe into the river. "Come on in! Dive to the bottom of the river," he said. "That's where the water is the coolest. Go down, open your mouth, and drink."

It was the strangest sensation, drinking at the bottom of a river, but he was right, It was cool and refreshing. It wasn't until I surfaced that I realized what we had done.

"Are we crazy? We just caught a piranha!"

Gerson grinned. "Oh, those stories are greatly exaggerated. Trust me." He laughed and vaulted back into the canoe. We stopped alongside the river at the hut of a Sateré family, and they let us use their fire to roast our fish. Boy, did it taste good!

Back at the village we sat down to talk to Márcia in the shade of Cadete's home. "You know, Jim," she said, "we live totally differently out here. You probably noticed we didn't have breakfast. The villagers haven't eaten lunch, either. We live just like the Indians do. Sometimes we go a whole day without eating, then someone catches something or traps something and we eat.

"One day I started out early in my canoe, visiting all the dwellings I could, inviting the Sateré to a special church meeting. By the time I got back, most had arrived, and we began the service. It lasted at least seven hours. By the time I crawled into my hammock it was about 2 a.m. I was so hungry. I hadn't eaten all day. I prayed, 'Lord, thank You for the good meeting with the Saterés, but I'm so tired and hungry. Would it be too much to ask for something to eat?'"

Márcia was just about to go to sleep, she said, when Cadete's wife woke her. "She took me to the chief's fire and gave me two gourds. One was heaped with wild mushrooms, and the other was filled with fat ants, toasted until they were crisp."

I gulped. "How were they?"

"Oh, okay, I guess. A little spicy," Márcia said, laughing.

We met with the Indians that night. Afterward, the girls told us about other villages in desperate need of help. Márcia had just completed a trip to another group from the Sateré tribe—the village of Koruatuba.

"A year ago the people in this village killed a missionary by pouring burning oil on her," Márcia said, "but I felt I should try to reach them anyway. I took a twelve-year-old Indian girl with me. Elci stayed to continue our work here."

The journey took several days, and when Márcia and the Indian girl arrived at the village, the Indians refused to speak to them. They wouldn't even let them hang their hammocks in one of the huts.

"Instead they took us into the jungle where several deserted old huts were. The two of us stayed there all alone for two weeks. Whenever we went into the village, they shunned us." Márcia said she wasn't afraid of snakes in that deserted place, but she was frightened of jaguars, since they eat people.

"After two weeks," she continued, "a woman came out to us, bearing an offering of fish. Another brought us birds' eggs, and a third brought manioc. Then the whole village came. Now they acted friendly, and several of them asked, 'Didn't the devil come to you?' I found out they had us sleeping in the burial place for their babies. When we stayed out there without either dying or becoming insane, they figured we had greater spiritual power than the devil."

I sat there after Márcia's story, watching the Indians going about their chores. These two young girls who came from middle-class Brazilian families were out here alone in the jungle for months with these Indians. They were so brave—real missionary heroines! How could people ever think Brazilians wouldn't make good missionaries?

During our stay in the Atuka area, five chiefs came from other villages to ask Gerson and me, "the big chiefs of YWAM," to send missionaries to them as well.

One night the Indians persuaded us to go night fishing. They wanted to use our flashlights to help them see the fish to spear. It was a very difficult job for a newcomer, since the light refraction in the water misled you as to the fish's actual location. About 2 a.m., I gave someone else my flashlight and sat in the back of the canoe, relaxing and enjoying the night sounds. A fellow in the front named Alcir was pulling our canoe through a very marshy spot.

Our canoe was bumping against this log—*katonk, katonk, katonk.* I felt uneasy; something was wrong.

"Alcir," I called, "shine that light back here, will you?" When he did, I stared into the eyes of a snake on the edge of a log inches from my left arm, poised to strike. Alcir turned off the flashlight.

"Alcir!" I whispered urgently, "turn that light back on...pick up your spear and kill the snake!" I stayed as still as I could.

Then Alcir seemed to wake out of a dream and sprang into action. He slammed the blunt side of the spear against the snake. It drew its head back. He hit it again and again. Finally, the snake was a bloodied mass. I let out my breath. The Indian then told us that this snake was the deadliest kind in the jungle.

When I came home after thirty days in the Amazon, Pam showed me a letter. It was from someone at the YWAM base in Tyler, Texas. Two different intercession groups had felt led to pray that God would "spare Jim Stier's life in the Amazon." I had lost track of the days in the jungle, but it seemed very possible that they had prayed on the very day of my encounter with the snake.

Pam had some other news, too. She was pregnant again. This pregnancy was difficult, but not as bad as the first two. A little girl was born, and we named her Rachel.

We heard that the base in the north had taken in a baby boy. They weren't really set up to care for him and needed to find a home. Could our orphanage take him? With thirty children, our orphanage was overflowing. Pam and I prayed and felt that the baby in Belém was another gift from God for us. We adopted him, naming him David. Now we had five children—three white ones, plus a darling little black girl and a tiny boy with a good mix of Indian blood. I hoped our ministry would be as fruitful as our family.

Some of the staff went to start bases around Brazil. Jaime Araújo, now married to a girl named Maristela, went to the northeast and started a ministry in Recife amid great difficulties, demonstrating courage and faith. Another went south to start a YWAM center in Florianópolis. In Pôrto Alegre, Paulo Sergio and the team purchased a beautiful property entirely from Brazilian donations and staffed only with South Americans. Rui and Marilac started several house churches in Pôrto Alegre from their many converts.

Much of our dream was coming true. We now had five operating locations. In nine years we had trained hundreds of young missionaries, and had 250 full-time staff. Sometimes it was hard to understand how it was possible, but it was happening.

However, we needed a breakthrough soon in Belo Horizonte. The crowding and lack of progress on construction were wearing people down and limiting our growth. We had one hundred people on the Belo base, but our buildings were still in a primitive state after six years of being on the property. Most of the rooms had no plaster or paint. It had been so long since we had dug the foundations for our big building that the holes had eroded. It was depressing.

Then an American missionary from another organization came to teach at our school. It was dinnertime, and our people were lining up outside the cook house with their plates, as usual. After they got their food, they sat on the ground outside or on unused construction blocks, or they took their plates inside to their dorm rooms. My missionary friend and I found a couple of chairs and took our food over to a shady spot.

"Jim," he began as soon as we started eating, "I've been praying for you."

"That's good, Bob, I appreciate that."

"The Bible says, 'Hope deferred maketh the heart sick.'"

"And...?"

"Well, I can see you've got a great group here, but you really have to do something better for your workers. It's a leader's responsibility, you know, to give them a nice place to live."

I couldn't deny what he said. I nodded dumbly. His words hurt, making me feel guilty. What did he think I could do about it? I was doing the best I could. I was only one person. A couple of weeks later, another leader outside our mission came to me with virtually the same concern. He, too, was someone I respected.

Then, a few days later, George Foster taught at our school. No one had been better friends to us than George and Dolly Foster. George and I were walking around the property. I showed him where the trench for the big building's foundation was eroding.

"You really need more room, don't you, Jim?"

"Yeah, we sure do."

"Where do you put everybody?"

"The families each have one room. For the singles, we have bunks. It's pretty crowded."

"You need to do something better for your workers, don't you? I think it would help their self-esteem if they had better rooms...and a dining room to eat in."

I could hardly believe it. In four weeks' time, three men whom I respected had delivered the same bruising message. I knew it was true, but that didn't make it any easier to face. Just before dawn the next day, I went on top the flat roof of my unfinished office. It was a good place to pray, set off in a more wooded part of the property. I paced back and forth on the roof in the crisp, cold air, pouring out my complaint to God. The sky started to lighten with the coming day as I wrestled in prayer, fighting for a breakthrough. Then a thought came to me. Maybe I had carried the struggle as far as God wanted me to. It was time to give it to Him.

"Father, You heard what these people said. But YWAM in Brazil wasn't my idea, Lord. You've led us every step of the way. This is Your responsibility. I'm just Your servant. I will do whatever You show me, but this isn't mine to take care of." I looked out over the property and our pitiful collection of half-finished buildings.

"This is Your mission, Lord. We need to finish these buildings, but only You can make it possible."

TWENTY-THREE

From the Land of Dreams and Visions

SOMETHING crystallized in me that morning. I left my place of prayer feeling lighter than I had for a long time. Ten days later, George came back. He had a check from all our friends in Betânia...$1,500. That could get us started again. Bless them!

Then John Dawson, a leader of YWAM for the western part of the United States, came to Brazil to speak at our annual missions conference. John and I had been friends since my earliest days with YWAM, and it was great seeing him again. On his way to the airport after his time with us, John surprised me with a prediction.

"God has told me something, Jim. When I get back to the States, the next church I'm speaking in is going to help you."

Sure enough, I got a letter a few weeks later from Russ Doty, an associate pastor of Christian Chapel in Walnut, California. John had spoken at their church and told them about our work, and they wanted to know what they could do to help.

I got back to him right away, asking if they could send a construction team to help us finish our big building. Six months later twenty-four volunteers arrived. And they brought $10,000 with them for construction materials! All our people pitched in, and in the next two weeks we finished the meeting hall/dining room and a second floor above for dormitories. When our new friends from California left, they promised to come back the next year for another project.

I stood in the middle of what had been built and thanked God. "Lord, You did it. Thank You for sending those wonderful people from the States. Give us more partners like them. Help us send out more Brazilian missionaries. And help us always make this a place that bolsters the dignity of those You bring to us, Lord."

I was learning something through all this. It seemed we would always be in a battle, but even in the midst of the worst struggles, I could let God carry the load. One by one, the Lord gave us others to stand by us financially. We finally completed the buildings and threw ourselves with new vigor into the ongoing ministry. We were determined to see our dreams come true, including sending Brazilians around the world.

Meanwhile, we were doing more than ever to proclaim the gospel in Brazil. The outreach at the spiritist festival in Rio mushroomed. After the first three years, the Brazilian churches got more and more involved. It peaked when ten thousand Christians came one New Year's Eve to preach and witness up and down the beach.

Of course this didn't sit too well with the spiritists. They started having trouble getting their "guides" to possess them. Little wonder, what with all the angelic activity on Copacabana Beach! I heard a TV news anchorman report, "This New Year's Eve the beaches belonged to the Christians."

New bases had been started in Rio de Janeiro, Curitiba, Blumenau, and Manaus. When a young couple arrived from Holland to work with the street children, that ministry took root and blossomed. Johannes and Jeanette soon had a team working among the hard-core street kids. I remembered when Pam and I were with

George Foster just after first arriving in Brazil and saw our first street kid. Now we were making a difference in scores of these kids' lives, getting them off drugs and off the streets.

Our staff was now five hundred strong. Outreaches like Rio were happening throughout the year all around Brazil. Rui's work had grown to more than twenty churches with more than two thousand new believers. We were ministering to communities and Indian tribes in various parts of the Amazon and had developed about thirty linguists along the way. We still lived on the brink of total disaster financially, but by now that seemed almost normal. I hoped I was finally learning to trust the Lord more.

Despite all this, I still heard the echo of what I had told those doubtful missionaries at the conference when we first arrived in Brazil: "We want to mobilize and train Brazilian young people for world evangelism."

✿ ✿ ✿ ✿

A few Brazilians had gone out from our base to other continents, but there had been very few. We were having an impact on Brazil and the neighboring countries, but it wasn't enough. There were very real barriers to overcome—most of our workers only spoke Portuguese, and the Brazilian economy now suffered from a 1,000-percent annual inflation rate. But somehow we had to do it.

A few of our people started studying English. Then we held a special leadership course for our key staff. During the three months of intensive training, each student had to develop a project with a two-year plan showing how he or she would initiate a ministry either in Brazil or overseas.

Loren Cunningham came and spoke for our leadership school. While teaching, he mentioned there were only two countries in the world where YWAM had never ministered. One was Pitcairn Island in the Pacific, and the other was a small Portuguese-speaking country called São Tomé e Príncipe. The former Portuguese colony was located off the coast of West Africa. Robson Soares, one of our young married men, came to me a few days later. Robson was always like a coiled spring, full of enthusiasm and energy. Now he looked as if he was about to burst.

"Jim," he said, "you are going to really like my project for the school! I'm not just writing a school paper. I'm going to actually *do* my project!"

"What is it?"

"I'm going to do the research and formulate a plan for evangelizing São Tomé e Príncipe…then I'm going to recruit a team and do it!" he declared, sounding as satisfied as if it were accomplished.

Was this the moment? I faced this energetic young man and wondered for an instant if it was too much, too soon. I decided to test his resolve. "That's a Communist country, Robson. They won't allow us to preach the gospel there."

"I know, but there has to be a way," he insisted.

"It's a very poor place. I've been reading about it. Your health will be in constant jeopardy. Food will be hard to buy."

"I realize all that, but I think God wants us to do it."

"Do you think you will be able to come up with money for the airline tickets and support after you are there?"

"It will be hard, but I think we can do it."

I stood looking at Robson. He seemed so full of faith. For years I had dreamed of Brazilian teams going out like this. Robson and his wife, Lucimar, were so young, though, and had no international experience. Then I remembered Pam and myself, years before. How had our leaders been able to trust us with so much? Didn't Robson and Lucimar deserve the same chance?

"Okay, Robson, let's go for it."

We developed a plan during the rest of the school, and then Robson went to work. First, he would make a reconnaissance trip to São Tomé e Príncipe with a friend. He sold some property he owned to pay for their tickets. The two young men came back full of enthusiasm. I began to feel my own heart quicken. Something was emerging from the land of dreams and visions. It was really happening.

Robson soon had a team of fourteen volunteers, plus three children. The Brazilian church responded to his appeals, and many of the team members were able to raise the needed financial support. It looked as though they could leave Brazil toward the end of the year. We didn't want to do this in a corner, so we set up a missions convention for November. Two thousand attended the last night. John Dawson was with us and gave strong prophetic encouragement to the group. We had the whole team, plus their pastors, come forward. We laid hands on each one and prayed for them, commissioning this first group of Brazilian YWAMers to go out and start a permanent work to spread the gospel in an overseas nation. They were heading for one of the most needy and difficult corners of the world, but I could see only joy and determination on their faces. I could almost hear the unseen fortresses of the enemy collapsing.

Epilogue

T H R E E months after our young team of missionaries left Rio for their assignment in Africa, I flew from Brazil to São Tomé e Príncipe to visit them. It was night when we circled the landing strip, and I could barely make out a few dim lights below.

The hot, humid air hit me as I stepped off the plane and made my way to a small, pink stucco and brick building—the smallest international terminal I had ever seen. I inched through the crowd of sweating Africans and Russians who were waving passports and yelling at officials on duty behind dirty glassed-in booths. There was no attempt to form an orderly line.

I advanced through passport control, on to customs, then to the baggage area where people elbowed each other as they tried to claim their bags. I emerged dripping wet. *If it is this hot at night, what would noon feel like?* I wondered. Then I saw Robson and the team, waving and cheering despite the sweltering heat. I ran toward them and was greeted by a round of hugs and a chorus of welcomes. Several Africans, smiling broadly, encircled us.

"Jim, meet our friends," said Robson. "These are some of our converts."

We exchanged damp handshakes, then climbed onto an old flatbed truck that Robson had borrowed. The team had been here for three months and still had no vehicle.

As we rumbled through the deserted streets, Robson filled me in on their progress. Many people were being saved from virtual paganism. Only a few hundred Christians lived in this country of 140,000 but the number was growing weekly. The small evangelical church seemed very happy with the missionaries' work. The people were open to the gospel, and their enthusiasm sometimes bordered on dangerous! "Once we tried to hand out tracts in a praça downtown," Robson recounted. "So many people wanted our materials that they mobbed us. One of our guys was almost trampled. He was the one with the tracts! We had to drag him out."

We made our way through silent streets, and I noticed that the buildings resembled Brazil's, but even poorer. "Robson, how do you get around here?" I asked.

"We walk, or we hitch rides. It's hard to find a taxi, but many private cars stop and give rides for a small price. Actually, we're famous all over São Tomé as the only foreigners who always hitch rides. Sometimes, when we're out of money, we walk three or four hours to our meetings."

He told me they had started six small groups of believers. About two hundred now followed Christ and regularly attended the sessions.

We drove into the hills above the city and parked in front of a wooden house set on columns. We climbed fifteen concrete steps and walked into the three-bedroom house that was home to two married couples, three children, and ten single adults. This was YWAM, São Tomé e Príncipe.

I joined them for the next several days, hitching rides to get to the various settlements. We walked from house to house inviting people to our meetings. After we had gathered a few dozen, we'd have a service. Every time, someone would make a decision for Christ—usually several people.

The team was holding up physically, although Robson said most had suffered bouts of malaria. A large percentage of the population had the disease, and during rainy season many children died. Food was scarce, and our team had been existing on breadfruit, jackfruit, and fish.

On Wednesday evening—our night off—we closed the house tightly at five o'clock to protect ourselves from malaria-bearing mosquitoes. The house was as hot as a sauna inside. We gathered under the single dim light bulb: Robson, myself, and a couple of others sitting on rough, homemade wooden benches. A knock came at the door, and since I was the closest, I answered it. Four young Africans stood in the early evening darkness.

"My name is Bandeira," said the tallest one in melodic, African-accented Portuguese. He was a strong, handsome young man. "These are my friends. We heard you know about Jesus. We have never had a chance to learn about Him. Will you tell us?"

I ushered them into our primitive living room and motioned them to a bench. We sat in the oppressive heat and talked for several hours. Although it was dark and uncomfortable and my shirt clung to my back with sweat, I felt a tremendous privilege to be there, telling these young men about the Lord. They were quick to comprehend. Bandeira, especially, was like a hungry man discovering food.

Before they left, they suggested that we meet again on Saturday— this time to play soccer. The competitive Bandeira, a popular player on a local team, was eager to demonstrate his soccer skills to Brazilians. On Saturday we kept our date, played with Bandeira and his friends, and had a great time. In only a few days I had grown to love these new friends, especially Bandeira. Someday I knew he would become a Christian.

After I returned to Brazil, Robson wrote regularly, reporting the group's progress. They were soon telling of more than four hundred converts and more villages with more groups of believers. Then came the news I had anticipated. Bandeira had made his decision for Christ.

Reports from our team in São Tomé stirred excitement in others. Teams prepared to leave for Macau, next to Mainland China, and Guinea-Bissau in Africa. Others began talking of launching similar efforts in Indonesia, Albania, Angola, and Mozambique. I wrote to Robson and told him that he and his team had broken down barriers and had set an example that was inspiring other Brazilians to attempt dreams that they earlier considered impossible.

Then sad news arrived. I sat down one afternoon to open my mail. Among the letters was one with a São Tomé stamp—from Robson. I opened it first. A cholera epidemic had broken out in São Tomé. Bandeira was the first of their friends to fall victim.

"He came to see us one evening, and he was excited because he was going to take his examination the next day to qualify as a schoolteacher," wrote Robson. "Before he left, I asked him a question. 'Bandeira, how is your soul? How are you with Jesus?' He smiled and answered, 'Great! Really great! I'm full of joy in Jesus.'

"Hours later he was dead."

I put down the letter for a minute, thinking of that strong young man, laughing and kicking the soccer ball in the sunshine. Robson described Bandeira's memorial service that drew one thousand people. "I performed the funeral, Jim. I preached Jesus to all those people. It was the largest public gospel meeting in São Tomé since independence... maybe the largest one ever."

Robson also told how the cholera epidemic was still raging. No medical supplies were available, and almost everyone who contracted the disease died. Our team could hear the moans and shrieks of people in the agonies of impending death. The epidemic was centered in their neighborhood, and many of their friends died.

"When the woman who sold us bread every morning died of cholera, we thought we would die, too," wrote Robson. "A terrible darkness settled on the land. We got up each morning, shaking with fear as we joined hands to pray. Then we went out as usual to minister to the people."

Besides their regular activities, they attended an average of three funerals a day. They never stopped praying with people, comforting them, and telling them about Jesus. By now more than ten groups of believers met regularly. Our base in Belo Horizonte began to pray intensely that God would spare their lives and make them even more fruitful.

I visited them again within a few weeks. The cholera epidemic had run its course, life was almost normal, and Robson and his team met me with more converts in tow.

One morning I walked into the heavy tropical growth behind the team's house to find a place to pray. Although it was early, the air was hot and sticky as I settled down on a log. I brushed away mosquitoes that hummed around my ears.

"Thank You, Lord, for all You've done here," I whispered. "You are so faithful!" I thought about what I had witnessed and heard on this visit. I remembered Bandeira and the hundreds who had come to know Jesus since my young soccer friend had died. I was proud of our team's accomplishments. In fourteen months they had faced incredible difficulties and had prevailed. Their struggles had been much greater than those Pam and I had faced when we arrived in Brazil fifteen years earlier.

I remembered the distinguished old missionary in his white tropical suit, telling me that God hadn't called Brazilians to be missionaries. I recalled all the other leaders who had echoed that belief as we told them about our dream. So many had tried to convince us it was impossible! How I wished they could see these courageous pioneers. Robson and his team were the best missionaries I knew.

I got up from the log and dusted off my clothes. As I walked back to the house, I felt faith surge in my heart. We would see waves of Brazilians going out all over the world. We would see not only Brazilians, but Africans and Asians, too. The sacrifice had been worth it. The difficulties were part of the process, part of the privilege. I couldn't wait to see what the next decade would bring.

I smiled as I remembered the new converts here in São Tomé sharing how God was calling them to become missionaries. Of course, many people argued that the economy cannot support missions; that the people of São Tomé aren't cut out to be missionaries....

For more information on YWAM in Brazil, write:
Jovens Com Uma Missão
Caixa Postal 2024
30.161 Belo Horizonte, Brazil

Donations should be sent to:
Youth With A Mission
P. O. Box 4600
Tyler, TX 75712-4600

Checks should be made payable to Youth With A Mission, with a note enclosed specifying how you want the gift to be used.

Christian Heroes: Then & Now

Adventure-filled Christian biographies for ages 10 and up!

Readers of all ages love the exciting, challenging, and deeply touching true stories of ordinary men and women whose trust in God accomplished extraordinary exploits for His kingdom and glory.

Available from YWAM Publishing
1-800-922-2143
www.ywampublishing.com

Also available: Christian Heroes Unit Study Curriculum Guides